Descendents of Richard Freemantle 1820 South African Settler

Focusing of the line of

John Mates Freemantle = Doris Rona Boshoff

With acknowledged extracts from:

John Mates Freemantle, Ruth Frances May (nee Freemantle), Serena De Jager, David Freemantle and a letter from John's sister:
Extract from: Olive Penfold, the daughter of Oliver Woodland Freemantle, who married (1st) Muriel Selina Goldsmith and (2nd) Dorothy Frances Mates - letter dated 20.2.1989.

Descendants of Richard Freemantle 1820 South African Settler

"NEITHER BY ENTREATY NOR REWARD"

Lesley Moseley (nee Boshoff)

This little project started with renewed contact with my late father Louis Boshoff's brother-in-law, my Uncle John Freemantle. One day I just decided to get in back in touch and he was thrilled to hear from me.

I told him I had been publishing books and he asked me if I would publish his manuscript, showing the Freemantle family tree, specifically relating to an ancestor Richard Freemantle, who had gone to South Africa as one of the 1820 Settlers. I readily agreed.

However, when the 'manuscript', arrived it was a printout of a Genealogy web-site download, compiled by Selena De Jager. I then found another download by Ruth Francis May (nee Freemantle).

I have endeavored to get permission from these ladies, but I have spent hours editing the information and as this is not a commercial venture, feel sure that as its data in the public domain, and a gift for an elderly man, nobody would refuse.

The letter from the late Olive Penfold (nee Freemantle), Uncle John's sister, details incidents of their shared childhood memories.

JOHN MATES FREEMANTLE

*(Extracts from his son David Freemantle's memoirs
as recorded covering mostly years 1945-1972)*

John:

When I came back from the war in late 1945, I went back to work for the railways in Johannesburg. I was working at the railway headquarters' in Johannesburg as a clerk. My job there was in advertising vacancies in a newspaper.

My job was to get the information from the applicants and summarise them and put them on a form to be sent to the railway head quarters in Pretoria. They then selected the applicants for the job vacancies.

As we came back from the war, the Natts treated ex soldiers very badly. They treated us as enemies; they called us red louses '*rooi lussie*'.

When we volunteered to go overseas, the Natts were pro German. Smuts supported the war effort and as soldiers who volunteered to go overseas, we had to sew red shoulder flashes on our uniforms. The Afrikaner's called us '*rooi lussie*'. Lussie actually translates as strips.

(*extract of unknown origin*)

" *During the Second World War, South Africa's Prime Minister, Jan Smuts, had built up a reputation as an Internationalist, particularly during the formation of the United Nations. As Smuts had supported Indian Home Rule and was privately considering dismantling segregation in South Africa, many poor whites, particularly unskilled workers, switched their votes to the National Party, believing that increased black migration to the cities would have a devastating effect on their livelihood.*

D.F.Malan had strong Afrikaner roots and was able to capitalize on that fear, particularly as most of Smut's cabinet was made up of English speaking South Africans who had little sympathy for Afrikaner interests. Living costs during the Second World War had risen by almost half; real wages were also down for whites but had risen for blacks.

The South African general election of 1948 was held on the 26 May 1948 and saw Herenigde Nasionale Party leader DF Malan call for the prohibition of mixed marriages, for the banning of black trade unions and for stricter enforcement of job reservation. Running on this platform of apartheid,as it was termed for the first time, Malan and his party benefited from the weight given to rural electorates, defeating Smuts and his United Party. Smuts even lost his own seat of Standerton. Also 90% of UP seats were urban renamed itself the National Party and ruled South Africa until 1994 "

John:
The Herenigde Nasionale Party and its coalition partner, the Afrikaner Party, won seventy-nine seats against the seventy-four of their United and Labour Party opponents, although the Herenigde Nasionale Party had received 140,000 less of the total votes cast than their opponents. The Herenigde Nasionale Party consequently became the government

Many of the nationalists were detained during the war in concentration camps this added to their dislike of the English. When any ex army blokes applied for the jobs then they had to sit a test.

The test was taken in a room in my office; my boss used to run the test. Anyone who applied for a job or a promotion had to sit the test. They brought them to the office and were given a set of books, English, Afrikaans dictionary, sat them down, and if they were English they had to write a letter in Afrikaans. If you were a Dutchman, it did not matter if you passed or not. However, if you were English speaking and you failed the test you did not get the job. It was because of this and other factors eventually it got so bad that I said to hell with this.

I started to look around for alternatives' and found an advert for a job in Rhodesia.
I had been trained as a clerk and taught myself to do shorthand. I obtained an interview and took leave to go up to Gwelo. I arrived in Gwelo early morning just after midnight and I slept in the waiting room until morning. I walked down to the council office, which was a little way down from the station, and the town clerk interviewed me and I was given the job.

Consequently, I arranged to go back to Johannesburg and gave in my notice. I loaded my furniture and my family and moved to Rhodesia by train. I unloaded my furniture off and arrived at a council house in Gwelo. I was there for a while and eventually moved to another house one of these pise dtere houses. A pise house had rammed earth walls of mud and a thatched roof. These houses were built because there was a shortage of housing and were cheap and easy to build; pise means house and dtere means of mud.
The doorframes and doors were made of wood and of course, the white ants loved it and with a roof of thatching.
The council had quite a few of them. At one stage, I actually bought one. I started fixing it up and I put a new doorframe and door in because the white ants had gotten to it. However, it was quite a time.

These houses were not very big just like a big mud hut really at one time, people.
I was to take over from another stationmaster who was being transferred to Rutenga station. When he handed over to me the only instruction he gave me was that a company called Brown and Root, was responsible for the building of a mine in Selebi-Phikwe. He told me that this was going to be a big operation and they had a man there who was to look after their records. He told me that this company was going to handle thousands of tons of construction materials for the building of the new township at Selebi Phikwe mine site to house some several hundreds of families.
They had a few mining engineers' from Johannesburg, whose job it was to sink the mine shaft and there was going to be an awful lot of equipment coming by rail mainly from Rhodesia even though in those days there was sanctions on Rhodesia. The cement and stonework required for building the mineshaft was to be unloaded at Serule station and shipped out to the mine site by road some 60 klm away in the bush.
Now when he told me this I looked at what I had and as a stationmaster there, how I would handle that. There was absolutely nothing there, no siding nothing, just a little spur that you could use as a siding but it was very small, only a couple of hundred meters long.

As a result, I got onto my superiors in Bulawayo to the promotional section there and advised them of what was happening.

I suggested that they send someone out to establish exactly what was required in the way of handling this equipment. Consequently, they came, had a look at it, and went back to Bulawayo.

As a result I was left to look after the station; my station consisted of a small station building made of wood and iron, and across the road a bit, a building that was used for relief staff.

There were four railway houses on the side of the track, which was the whole of Serule. There was a big underground water tank that was filled by water from the Shashe River, which came down by rail tank cars, which was decanted into this underground tank, and was pumped up to a pumping station above ground to reticulate the area.

These tank cars would come round periodically and sent back for more water from the Shashe River from a sand pump there.

As a result, after going back and forth to HQ about the problem, they decided to organise a two line siding that was connected up to a loop line along the side of the station yard and fenced it off, so that we had a place to store everything.

It took a little while to build of course but traffic started coming.

The first thing that came was the building equipment for the houses in the form of door and window frames for several hundred houses, these were stacked on the side of the loop line and came in three or four truck loads every day or so from Bulawayo.

They unloaded them on the side of the track, as there was nowhere else to put them. They were piled more than head height. Then they were carted away by road to the mine site where the builders had started to lay out the town site, which was quite a considerable town site and included a couple of stores.

All of the supplies for the mine site had to come by rail then shipped by road to Selibe Phikwe. There were wagonloads of beer and other things like food. They also sent me wagonloads of cement that came from Bulawayo in bags.

The company had a bunch of Botswana labourers whose job it was to off load this stuff onto the trucks. Every morning a train would come up from Bulawayo and dump a load of cement off including bricks and some stone.

Some material was also coming up from South Africa by road train that also went out to the mine site. Eventually the siding was built and then they were able to push this stuff into the siding and offload from there.

We had many problems with offloading, as some of the bags were broken, and it was the rainy season turning the loading area in the siding into a quagmire of mud and cement. All this made it difficult for the shunting staff; to make things worse, the road to Selibe-Phikwe was still a gravel road and the combination of heavy traffic and rain had turned the road into a mud track blocking the road with stranded trucks.

Nevertheless, the place got busier, everything for the mine in the form of foodstuffs had to be shipped out; they came by tranship from Bulawayo and South Africa. The only goods shed I had was a tin shed on one side and a little stone one. Neither could hold much, this was my total storage space. My station was completely under sourced.

I had two Botswana 'boys' as station labourers whose job it was to cart stuff around. We often unloaded goods material onto the grounds of the station, as there was no room to put it anywhere else.

At the mining site, there was a considerable population of building staff plus mining engineers' and tradesmen to sink the shaft.

In the mean time, I had a staff of two station foremen and myself to run the station. The station foremen used to have every alternate weekend off; during which time the stationmaster had to act as the station foreman as well as being the stationmaster.

Later I had three station foremen to make it a bit easier. However, to start with I had to act as a relief station foreman on twelve-hour shifts every alternate weekend for station foremen that needed leave.

That was a very busy time because we had no shunting staff there and as I had goods traffic coming in which required shift work. I was shunting doing train's work, bookkeeping, selling tickets, keeping monthly records and so on.

Eventually I got a clerk, one of the blokes who were looking after the incoming mining and construction material for Brown and Root, his name was Ted. Ted was an oldish bloke in his fifties his wife came to stay with him from South Africa. She was much younger than he was she was in her thirties. She was hired to do some of the clerical work.

Brown and Root built him and his wife a small house adjacent to my station for him to use, as his office. It was just set of walls with a bedroom and a room for an office and a roof.

One of the local Tiswana chief's who lived over the hill a short distance away from Serule, had an arrangement with the railway staff to provide them with a couple of cows in milk in exchange for a few rand a month.

They would put the cows and their calves in a kraal that they had built behind the staff housing.
First thing in the morning, we would milk the cows then let them out to graze nearby keeping the calves in the little kraal. Then in the evening when the cows came home to feed their calves, we would milk them again before they feed the calves.

Whenever one of the cows ran out of milk they contacted the chief he would take it away and replace it with another cow that was in calf.

That is how we got fresh milk, as there was no store at the station at all; the nearest store was way down the line in the next town we were really stuck in the bush.

Apart from selling tickets and delivering goods coming in for people living in the area and arranging for bits and pieces to be sent away for one reason or another as a stationmaster, it was also my responsibility to release pigeons' as a regular thing. Every so often, several hundred odd pigeons in cages would come down by train from racing pigeon clubs in Bulawayo and released.

One day a Tiswana woman came to the station and brought in a pigeon and gave it to the station foreman, she said she found. The station foreman said that he would send it back to Bulawayo by train. Next day she came back and wanted to claim money from the station foreman for this pigeon as she thought that she should get a reward for handing it in. Because of not getting a reward, a Botswana police officer came down to question the station foreman and arrest him for thieving.

Luckily we talked him out of that but the old lady insisted that she wanted some money for saving the pigeon she expected something in return for it. Eventually they disappeared and the police officer did not arrest the station foreman, it was very close because as Rhodesians we were a bit on the nose in regards to the Botswana people.

Another incident that happened at Serule station while we were there was the accidental death of one of a local Tiswana woman. We had a water tap next to the station building that the local villagers used to collect clean water. The Tiswana woman would line up each with a little bucket on their head, stand in a queue, and fill the bucket from the tap.
After filling their bucket, they would walk back to their kraal over the hill. An hour or so latter they would be back again and stand in a queue, this would go on all day long, and I thought to myself what are they doing with all that water.

One day while the shunting was going on one of these 'nannies' was accidentally struck and severely injured by one of the railway wagons when she tried crossing the railway line. She was not aware of the moving wagons when the shunter signalled the locomotive driver to come back and shunted into her.

She was rushed to Francistown hospital where she in due course died. This incident caused a big kafuffle since it took a long time to work out the recompense for the woman that had been killed because of her injuries.

At the time, my daughter Rosemary who was a nurse was visiting us at the time. She did all she could to help but the woman's injuries were too severe and eventually died.

I had my hands full of real problems, human problems and quite a few problems of various kinds while I was there like when a goat drowned in the water supply.

The water supply consisted of a concrete underground reservoir located next to spur line. This had a cement runway that ran parallel to the tracks; this had an opening with a metal lid on it in the center to fill the tank with water. Then one day we found many flies around it.

Consequently, we opened up the water tunnel to get to the underground tank and down inside where a dead goat, which had climbed in when the hatch was open. The goat had tried to get some water and after falling in had drowned.

As a result, we had to pump all the water out of the tank clean it, refill it again and put a few bags of lime in the water. For a while, everyone complained that the water tasted a bit meaty.

Incidentally, right next to the railway line, there were two graves from many years before, a stationmaster and station foreman were both buried there. The story was that the stationmaster and station foreman's wife was involved in a love tryst of some description resulting in them both being shot. They were then buried there; when they built the siding, they had to very careful not to dig up the graves.

Camped with us was a group of surveyors who were surveying the railway line to Selebi Phikwe laying out the track. There was a bit of fun and games with them as well. One of the station foremen's wives got involved with some of the surveyors and we had quite a job getting that sorted out.

Christmas 1971, Rene, one of the station foremen was supposed to be on duty at the station. Another who was off duty was having a party at his house. The third station foreman lived next door and was trying to sleep as he was on duty next. His wife came to me and complained about the noise that these people were making. I went round and as I opened the door the station foreman who was off duty came to the door with a beer in his hand, and Rene who was supposed to be on duty was there having a drink too.

This caused a confrontation between Rene and I. Rene

was an ex police officer from South Africa and was twice my size; he eventually went back to South Africa.

The next morning they came to me because they wanted to contact the office and complain about me, so I said 'right we will all go, and we can tell them the story, it's up to you'. They pulled back. For about a week, everybody used to pass each other like stinking fish. No one would talk to each other.

Rene, the story about him was that he was a very powerful person and we used to keep a station bicycle to go down and set the points that was about 150 meters away to let trains in and out. He was so powerful he damaged the bicycle pedals. He bent them so I got a new one to replace it. Within two weeks, I was using the old one to repair the new one. He was so strong the pedals just gave way.

Danny Kay was the stationmaster of Plumtree when dad was at Tesebe his first station in Botswana. Danny was a very handy bloke; he taught me a lot at the train's center. I used to work opposite him as a stationmaster as I had to do trains work as well.

In 1971, Plumtree School had just finished building a cinder track for our annual sports weekend; this was held towards the end of first term.

We slept here over night in the school in the dormitory with the other visitors for the long weekend sports weekend. Ian Smith was there. The beds were terrible; the woman in one dorm; men in the other. One of the women fell out of the bed. It was funny. The boys were feeding us in the morning and we went to the sports ground in the evening and we would get together for sundowners. Mrs. Janet Smith said we should smoke more because of our tobacco economy.

It was funny because there was a war on.
It was a confusing time. How did u feel leaving the boys there? When we went down for weekends we used to take the boys to the hotel.

We had a snake in the house hiding behind the fridge. I went for it with a broom tried to catch it but I bashed a hole in the cabinet trying to kill it. There on the linoleum it was still slithering around. It kept moving.

Another incident in Hunters Road was when a nanny came over to the house. She had cut herself on the crook of her arm rather badly with a tin can and dad had to sew her arm up. He had no real first aid kit and patched her up the best he could using an ordinary sewing needle and cotton thread.

David:
When we came home for school holidays, we often used to go to the store behind the house. It was on the main road. The shopkeeper had a dog that had puppies.

On this one occasion, Rosemary went in to the store just as the shopkeeper was yelling at the puppies. Rose who is so soft about animals did not like the way he treated them and gave him a mouthful. The shopkeeper told her that if she did not like the way he treated them then she could have them. Therefore, she took them both.

Yet again, we had acquired a couple more hind's ninety nines sausage dogs. We called one Minnie the other Chombe.

One of the local Africans did not like that and said, shaking his head in disapproval "Why you call him Chombe".

In the early 1960s, Mosa Chombe was an African activist from the breakaway Katanga province in the Belgian Congo Hence his disapproval in calling a dog Chombe.

We only had Chombe for a short while. Minnie we had for seventeen years; she died in Bulawayo were I buried her. She came upstairs to mom and looked at her then walked back downstairs, mom followed her, when she got to the bottom of the stairs she just lay down and died right there.

It was as though she came to say goodbye. I had the job of burying her. I buried her under the avocado tree in the garden back of the flats.

John:
At the time, I was working in a butcher shop. I had retired early, as we were getting ready to immigrate to Australia. I had to go back to work again as things were taking longer than expected.

I worked for a few months at the butcher shop it belonged to a German bloke; he and his wife lived in the flat just below us.

He they gave me a job to look after this shop. It was an African shop near Luveve township where the Africans came to buy their meat. My job was to monitor the meat as it came in and I had an African bloke who did the actual cutting of the meat. We used to get tripe and other offal as well. I was also responsible to keep track of the money.

Every time I came home from work mom (Doris) used to complain that I smelled like a butcher shop. I used to walk into the shop and think that his place stinks but after a few minutes, you do not notice it anymore.

When I came back from Serule to Bulawayo, I had a bit of money saved up and I decided to get a car. I was fifty or so at the time when I got my self a second hand car. It was a gray ford Corsair. I paid about 6 or 7 hundred dollars for it. I now had to learn how to drive a car so John and Rose taught me how to drive. I wanted to drive and I hoped when I went to Rhodesia that I could buy a car but could not afford it. Still, I went to the licensing place and there were hordes of Africans learning to drive, as they needed a license to drive their Kaffir taxies. I had to fit in with this lot and lessons and when I went for my driving test, I had to back into a set of drums and flour bags.

When I passed, my feelings were mixed. I knew that I could drive but the moment that they said that I had a license now I felt nervous. The very first drive I went on as a licensed driver I will never forget. I went as slow as I could, as I was a bit nervous it was a funny feeling as I was over fifty years old.
  I must have been the oldest learner driver they ever had as far as I was concerned.

I drove this car for quite a few years. Then June had a Renault 4 that I took over from her when they left for Australia. I rode that about to Gwelo and back to Bulawayo.

When we left for Australia, I sold the car to garage a Ford dealership Dullys. The bishop of our branch was the manager at this garage, brother Peter Marsberg.

(ed note : My Uncle John and Aunt Doris currently live in a retirement village in Mandurah, Western Australia. This book is an heirloom gift for him. Les, August, 2010)

Sister to **JOHN MATES FREEMANTLE**

Extract from: Olive Penfold, the daughter of Oliver Woodland Freemantle, who married (1ˢᵗ) Muriel Selina Goldsmith and (2ⁿᵈ) Dorothy Frances Mates - letter dated 20.2.1989.

I will tell you what I remember about my dad, Oliver Woodland Freemantle, (birthday 18ᵗʰ February). He spoke about fighting in the Boer War, he also fought in Delville Wood and I remember his telling us of the trench warfare, he suffered shrapnel wounds while he was over there, and during his leave in England he met my mother, Dorothy Frances Mates.

My mom had been engaged to a Canadian who was killed in the battle at Delville Wood, she was working in the army and her family entertained South African troops while they were in England. She met my dad, they became friends and it turned into love, he proposed and after the war my mom followed him to South Africa as a war bride.

My dad had been married before he went to France. There was only one daughter from this marriage, but we never heard of her again. My dad did many jobs in South Africa. He spent his early life working on all the National roads from the Cape right up to the Transkei when he was a road inspector.

This job took him to many towns, hence the fact that all the children were born in different places. Whilst he worked in the Transkei he learnt to speak a number of native languages, and he was very popular among the tribes.

Naturally he spent a lot of time away from his family, particularly once we got older and had to attend school.

My mother was a real pioneer, especially as she had so recently come out from England and having to be on her own so much. However, she got along well with everyone.

My dad was a wonderful husband and father and he loved my mother so much. I can remember in my latter years, when my dad was much older and had stopped travelling for his job, he settled down at home here in Cape Town.

He started growing mushrooms in our garage. A business friend supplied the money for seed etc.. He did very well; the idea was when the crop was ready my dad would supply it to an hotel in Wynberg. However, with only a bicycle at his disposal, he was unable to keep up with his deliveries. I am talking about the days before supermarkets and it was not common then to buy fresh mushrooms, as one does today. Although my dad was a very ordinary man, I am still very proud to say he fought in the Boer War and at Delville Wood. My uncle, Walter Freemantle, was a lawyer and I remember him attending the 'Bunga' in Umtata where we lived as children.

I did not have a lot of contact with my dad's family. My grandparents died long before we were born and I cannot remember anything special about them, except that my grandmother lived to be a very old lady.

P.S. As a child, I remember, every Armistice Day my dad would take out all his medals and polish them, then go to attend the service. (I cannot recall what happened to his medals after his death.)

*(end of extract from **Extract from: Olive Penfold, the daughter of Oliver Woodland Freemantle, who married (1ˢᵗ) Muriel Selina Goldsmith and (2ⁿᵈ) Dorothy Frances Mates - letter dated 20.2.1989.**)*

Descendants of Richard Freemantle
(Extract from a compilation by Selena De Jager)

The earliest Freemantle's traced from my family are two brothers in Portsea, near Southampton in England. Most of the Freemantle's mentioned below are decedents from the various 1820 settlers who immigrated to South Africa from Europe, mainly England.

It seems that Richard(1) may have lived in Southampton where he married his first wife Elizabeth and then moved to the greater London area after his marriage to his second wife Sarah where he remained until immigrating to South Africa.

One of the Family stories passed down the generations is that after his first wife's death, Richard(1) Freemantle turned to his housekeeper for comfort and eventually married her, this as you can imagine caused a big scandal, one simply did not marry the help!

This caused a rift between Richard(1) and his father who was totally outraged that his son could bring such shame to his family. Richard(1) moved his new wife and his three children from his previous marriage to London to escape the wrath of his father. Richard(1) was totally disinherited by his father.

It is thought that Richard(1) learned the skill of wheelwright and wagon maker while staying in London, because none of the other Merchants wanted to hire him because of his father's doing, so he had to learn a trade (which is most uncommon in the landed gentry) to put food on the table.

Richard (1) father's name was also Richard; he was a wealthy London Gentleman and Merchant, who also had a large home at Southampton. The two brothers mentioned above are Robert Freemantle and Richard Freemantle.

Robert the eldest married Hannah and they had two children Joseph (b. 16.08.1777) and James (b. 05.01.1780) in Headley, Hampshire.

Richard Freemantle married Anne and they had five children William (c. 29.03.1765), Helena (c. 08.09.1769), Richard (b. 1771, c. 28.06.1771), Samuel (c. 19.02.1777) in Headley, Hampshire.

Richard (1) Freemantle may have been Richard and Anne Freemantle's third child, nothing to confirm or dispute this has been found.

Richard (1) married his first wife Elizabeth Mitchell at St Mary's, Portsea, and Hampshire, England on the first November 1795, witnessed by William Bramoelle and Hannah Plummer.

Elizabeth Mitchell came from a wealthy, well to do family that was well established in the Hampshire area. Elizabeth Mitchell Freemantle died between 1809 and 1814, the rumor is that she never fully recovered from the strenuous birth of her third child. She left behind her husband, Richard (1) and three sons, Richard, John and Samuel.

In 1814, Richard (1) remarried Sarah Kent in 1814 in London. Sarah was born in December 1788/9. Sarah was rumored to have come from a good family that had fallen on hard times. She had to get a job as a housekeeper to support herself. In those days woman did not have many choices in the job market, they could chose between selling themselves as kept woman or woman of the street, or they could enter into service where you would work as a servant in the house of a wealthy family. The couple remained in London, where their two children, Eliza (b. 1815) and George (b. 1818) were born.

In 1819, in response to the Settlement Scheme for the Cape Colony, Richard (1) convinced Sarah that they must put their names on the list to be considered for Settlement in the Eastern Cape, South Africa. He most probably told her that here was the chance to regain what he had lost, a chance to be a landowner again to own a 100 acres (which was a lot of land in those days) and make a lot of money through farming.

A chance to escape the stigma that followed them, master that married servant and a chance for Sarah to be accepted as one of the respectable class. Sarah agreed and Richard (1) joined a Irish group lead by Thomas Mohoney.

Richard (1) and Sarah Freemantle and their children set sail from Portsmouth, England on 14th December, 1819, in the 'Northampton', arriving in Table Bay on 26 March, 1820. After replenishing supplies, with only group leaders and the deceased allowed off the ship, the Northampton then sailed for Port Elizabeth.

The Ship arrived in Algoa bay on the 30 April 1820. They landed at Fort Freedom on 1 May 1820.

The approximately 4-month journey on the Northampton was not a pleasant one. Shortly after setting sail the Ocean collided with the Northampton, their sails became entangled and the mast ropes, which had to be cut as the ships were in danger of sinking. Smallpox broke out and many children perished because of this disease. The ship also just escaped drifting on to the Goodwin Sands. There was a lot of trouble between the Captain and the settlers, Mahoney's party in particular. Some of the Settlers caused so much trouble that the captain ordered many of them, the Freemantles included, to be placed in chains.

The authorities decided to locate Mahoney's party by the Clay Pits on the banks of the Coombs River, a great distance from Grahamstown and most of the other settler locations. It is thought that the reason the authorities placed Mahoney's party in the furthest land lot was because of their quarrelsome attitudes.

Mahoney's Party was one of the first parties to have trouble from the local Xhosa tribes because they were situated at the edge of the clay pits. The Clay pits attracted large numbers of Xhosa, who used the clay to adorn their faces and bodies for traditional reasons such as initiation ceremonies.

The Xhosa received permission from the government allowing them access to the clay pits. Each time the Xhosa came to get clay at the pits they would steal the settlers cattle as well as their household goods, farming implements and people would go missing and be found later to have been murdered. The authorities knew that the location allocated to Mahoney's party was the most dangerous of all the locations, because of the proximity of the clay pits and were secretly regarded by the authorities as 'the forlorn hope of the settlement', in other words they were thought to be doomed. They were the first party to have members killed.

Mahoney's party reached Coombs River (then known as Kap River) on 10 December 1820. Once the Party was established Thomas Barrington took over responsibility of the Party because of Mahoney's frequent absents from the location because of building contracts. Most of the Party left the location by 1825, the land was then held entirely by Thomas Mahoney.

A recorded incident in 1821 when Richard Freemantle (2) with Thomas Wallace (aged 44, of Sephton's party) were arrested for not having a pass while being away from their location, and so were then discharged from their Party.

Richard(2) moved to Grahamstown and began to practice the trade of a wagon maker and wheelwright.
In 1822 Richard (1) and Sarah Freemantle had a son, Thomas.

In 1822 Mahoney sent Richard (1) Freemantle with his two sons, John and Samuel and Dick Wilton with his wagon for a load of firewood and poles.
 On the way back about two miles from the house, the Xhosa attacked the group. Richard Freemantle was stabbed to death; Samuel was wounded in the leg with an assegai (spear). John was stabbed right through his torso with a spear; Samuel was

trying to pull the spear out of his leg when John was stabbed.

John fell on Samuel driving the spear right through his leg just under the knee, narrowly missing his other leg. As soon as he pulled the spear out of his leg he went to his brother's aid, breaking off the spear he lifted his brother on to his back and ran with him the last mile to the house, while the Xhosa's were chasing Dick Wilton.

The group's shouting had raised the alarm with Mahoney's family who came to see what was going on and met Samuel Freemantle running with John on his back.

Samuel laid his brother down and while he was telling them the story, his brother died. Samuel himself was quite feint from the loss of blood.

When the Xhosa lost Dick Wilton, they went back to the wagon and stole the cattle and whatever else they wanted. Dick Wilton had a very narrow escape, he saw the Xhosa man throw the spear at him, he jumped out of the way, ran after it, and threw the spear back at him, but he missed, the Xhosa man tried to stab him but he the managed to knock him unconscious with his fist. He made it home that evening very bruised and tired, but thankful to be alive.

Samuel Freemantle was taken to the military post at the Clay Pits. A patrol was sent after the Xhosa and the cattle but they were unsuccessful.

The event of Richards death was recorded thus in Samuel's diary

Sam Freemantle His Book Sept. the 14, 1824 Richard Freemantle My father was Killed age 47 by the Kaffirs also John My Brother aged 16 yrs 10 months and 11 days. They departed this life 23 August 1822.

After Richards (1) death Sarah moved with the children to Grahamstown where she struggled to support herself and the children. She was forced to sell her needlework in September 1823 to support the family. Samuel eventually took her in and they lived with him until she remarried.

On the 6 February 1824, in Grahamstown Sarah Freemantle married Joseph Stevens, Rev. William Geary performed the service. Joseph Stevens was a settler in Waite's party on the 'Zoroaster' Joseph was a Husbandman.

The children were not happy with Sarah for marrying Joseph Stevens, and George refused to move with her after the marriage, he stay with Samuel and was eventually adopted into his family.
 It is not known if Eliza remained as well, or if she went with her mother.
Sarah had two more children, Joseph Stevens (born about 1825) and Isabella Stevens (born about 1827).

Sarah died in Grahamstown on 14 October 1862, at the age of 74.

Generation No. 2

1. Richard Freemantle (2) was the eldest son of Richard Freemantle (1) and Elizabeth Freemantle nee Mitchell. He was born in 1796 in England, he married Patience Ford on the 1 December 1823 in the Baptist Church in Grahamstown.

The ceremony was lead by Rev. William Geary and was witnessed by William Bear. Patience Ford was the daughter of Edward and Jane Ford, (her father was the head of Ford's party, from Wiltshire, who traveled out on the 'Weymouth.).

She was born in 1806/7 and came of a family of four children, two brothers, James (born1803) and John (born 1804) and a sister, Elizabeth* (born 1809).

On arrival in Albany, the Ford party was moved three times before their location was settled. It lay across the river from Mahoney's location.

It is thought that perhaps Richard(2) went across the river after he was discharged from the party to look for work at the Ford location and this is where he met Patience Ford

Patience was born in 1806 in Warminster England. She was only 17 when she got married. In November 1824 Richard(2) was working as a wagon maker in Grahamstown, on the 13.12.1824 he was licensed to trade at the Fort Wiltshire Fairs, then the following year , on 24 September 1825, he employed 2 immigrants.

On 10 November 1827, Patience gave birth to their first and only child William. William was baptized in the Baptist Church in Grahamstown. Patience died on 16 February 1828 in Grahamstown at the age of 22, William, her child was only 3 months old. She was buried at the Baptist Church in Grahamstown.

Richard Freemantle (2) got remarried on 18 December 1837 to Elizabeth Hanna Hall, at St. Mary's Anglican Church in Port Elizabeth. Elizabeth was born in 1816 in England, so she was 21 years old at her wedding. Elizabeth Hannah Hall was a daughter of Benjamin Hall and Francis Sophia Hall, (Settlers from Bath, Somerset in Wilson's party on 'La belle Alliance'.), Her father was a farmer and a carpenter and they lived in a house on West Hill, Grahamstown.

I could not find out why, but Richard (2) moved to Port Elizabeth sometime between 1832 and 1837, It is also presumed that his wife, Elizabeth Hannah Hall also came to live there in that time, but whether she came with her family or on her own is not known. Elizabeth gave birth to her first child, Ellen Anne Freemantle on 5 August 1838, at the age of 22 in Port Elizabeth. Her second child Frances Elizabeth Freemantle was born 10 February 1840, in Port Elizabeth.

A year later in 1841 Robert John Freemantle followed, also born in Port Elizabeth. Two years later came George Richard Freemantle born on 4 June 1843 in Port Elizabeth. He was born after his father had died. His birth certificate states: son of the late Richard Freemantle. He was baptised on 21 April 1844 at the Grahamstown Cathedral Abode in Port Elizabeth by the Colonial Chaplain, John Heavyside. Richard (2) died sometime at the end of 1843 and the beginning of 1844, the reason or the exact date of his death is unknown.

2. Samuel Freemantle(1) was the second son of Richard Freemantle(1) and his first wife Elizabeth Freemantle (nee Mitchell). He was born on 2 February 1802 in either Southampton or London, England. It is thought that from the age of thirteen until the age of 18, he lived in London with his Father, Stepmother, brothers and sister, until they immigrated to South Africa.

After his father's death, Samuel(1) moved his Stepmother and surviving siblings to Grahamstown and bought a house, he worked as a wheelwright. His stepmother and his siblings remained with him until Sarah remarried on 6 February 1824, to Joseph Stevens, the children were not pleased with this union and George refused to move, so he remained with Samuel(1) who eventually adopted him into his own family when he got married.

Samuel(1) got married on 10 April 1827, to Sarah Elizabeth Paxton in the Anglican Church in Grahamstown, the service was lead by Rev. Thomas Ireland. Sarah was the daughter of Jesse Paxton and Sarah Paxton (nee Froy), Settlers in John Dixon's party on the 'Ocean and were located at Waai Plaats on a source of the Kaffir Kraal River. Sarah was born in London, England on 6 April 1803.

It is strange to think that when the Ocean and Northampton collided Samuel (1) was on the one boat and Sarah was on the other.

Samuel (1) Sarah had ten children, the first eight were born in Grahamstown, the first John Freemantle (thought to have been named after Samuel's brother that died), was born 10 January 1828,followed by Lois Freemantle born 7 December 1829, then came Sarah Freemantle on 5 March 1832, Samuel (2) was next on 21 May 1833.

Emma Freemantle followed two years later on 12 April 1835, next came Charles Freemantle on 28 May 1837, followed three years later by Harriet Freemantle born on 18 May 1840, Elizabeth Freemantle followed on 13 May 1840, Jesse William Freemantle was next born 1 April 1844, in the Border Region (I don't know which border). Last was Jonathon Freemantle born in 1847.

There is a record of a Freemantle helping at Manley Mission; it is thought that this was Samuel and his family. By 25 March 1833, he had reopened his business and was working as a house painter and decorator. By 6 July1837 he had opened a grocery shop in Grahamstown, and the on 10 July 1837, He sold his property and his merchandise and returned to the painting business. On the 26 December 1844, he purchased a farm near Bathurst, Bradshaw's Location.

In 1849 Samuel and Sarah's eldest daughter and second child, Lois Freemantle, married Samuel Patten Impy, who was a shopkeeper in Fort Beaufort.
They had one son, George Samuel Impy, born 1850. In July 1851 on the way home to Fort Beaufort with four companions, rebel Hottentots on the Koonap Heights murdered Samuel Impy.

In 1852 their second daughter, Sarah, married Charles Benjamin Trollip, (son of Benjamin and Mary Trollip, Settlers in Sephton's party)
In 1855, their second son, Samuel at the age of 21, died in Grahamstown.

It was in March 1856; John (their eldest son) married Harriet Hannah Miller, (eldest daughter of John Miller, also a Settler in Sephton's party.)

Emma married Casper Henry Hartley at a unknown date, (son of William and Mary Hartley, Settlers in Calton's party). Casper became a printer and publisher in Kimberley.

Harriet married Reuben Goulding in Queenstown in 1860, (son of George Goulding and Sarah Goulding nee Pike, who were also Settlers in Calton's party)
Jonathan their youngest child died at a young age.
In 1864, Samuel and Sarah Freemantle left Grahamstown with their two sons', Charles and Jesse William, at this time Samuel's was 61 years old. By the end of 1864, they were farming at 'Klein Fontein' in the Cradock district.

On 27 March in either Cradock or Queenstown, their son Jesse William Freemantle (Willie) married Fanny Elizabeth Paxton (daughter of David Paxton and Harriet Matilda Paxton nee Painter).
Then, the last of their daughters, Elizabeth, married Jeremiah Woodland in 1870, in Cradock. It was at this daughter's house in Cradock, that Samuel Freemantle died on 3.4.1879 and his widow, Sarah Freemantle died in Cradock, probably at her daughter's house too, on 10.8.1879, just four months later.
Shortly before their deaths, their last unmarried child, Charles Freemantle, married Rachel McDonald on 27.8.1878 also in Cradock. Rachel was a widow with two children and there were four children from this marriage.

3. John Freemantle was the third child of Richard Freemantle (1) and Elizabeth Mitchell; he was born 7 October 1805 in England and immigrated to South Africa with his father and his stepmother.

He was murdered by Xhosa men on 23 August 1822, two miles from home while on a wood excursion with his father Richard (1) and his brother Samuel, his father died with him, Samuel managed to escape death and tried to save John by carrying him home but it was too late. John was buried at Coombs with his father.

4. Eliza Freemantle was the fourth child of Richard Freemantle(1) and the first with his second wife Sarah. Eliza was born in 1816 in London, England; she immigrated with her parents to South Africa at the age of 4.

After her father's death, she moved to Grahamstown, with her mother and siblings to live with her half brother Samuel. When Sarah, her mother was remarried in 1824 to Joseph Stevens, it is not clear if she went with her mother or remained with Samuel like her brother George.

On 9 July 1832 in the Anglican Church in Grahamstown, Eliza Freemantle married Thomas Derbyshire; he was a settler in Heyhurst's party on the 'John' and was located in Trappes Valley. Thomas was born 1790 and was a gardener from Liverpool, England.

Children of Eliza Freemantle and Thomas Derbyshire were:

5. George Freemantle was the fifth child of Richard Freemantle (1) and the second with his second wife Sarah Kent. He was born in London on 10 October 1818 and immigrated to South Africa with his parents as a two-year-old toddler.

After his father's death, they moved to Grahamstown and lived with Samuel. When his mother got remarried on 6 February 1824, in Grahamstown to Joseph Stevens, he refused to move with her so remained with Samuel and was later adopted by him it his family. Thomas King as a carpenter employed George.

On 14 April 1840 George Freemantle was married by Rev. J. Richards in Grahamstown to Elizabeth Ann Stillwell, (daughter of William Stillwell and Martha Stillwell nee Dove), this ceremony being witnessed by her sister, Marianne Stillwell. Elizabeth Ann Stillwell was born in Cape Town on 11.4.1822. Her parents came out to the Cape Colony as Independent settlers in the 'Garland', departing from London in December 1819, sailed into Table Bay in March 1820.

When George got married, he was a mason at Grahamstown. In 1841 their first child Marianne (named after Elizabeth's sister) was born, sadly she died 6 weeks later and was buried in the Methodist cemetery in Grahamstown.

The following year Louisa Ann was born on 11 February 1842, followed two years later by Mary Freemantle who was born on 11 June 1844, she died a month later on 23 July 1844.

Next came Sarah Elizabeth Freemantle born on 29 March 1846. The next child was Harriet Martha Freemantle born 16 September 1848.

Followed by George Richard Freemantle born 14 September 1850 in Somerset East. He died at the age of three on 18 July 1853 in Middelberg. Emily Lois Freemantle followed born 23 October 1852 in Cradock 3 years later. The rest of the children were born in Middleburg except the youngest.

Caroline Emma Freemantle was the next born November 1855, Edith Cecilia Freemantle followed born 18 August 1858, and she died the following month in September 1858.

In 1960, Edith Anne Freemantle was born 28 December 1860, and the Second Last child Maud (Martha) Eliza Freemantle was born 14 May 1864. Youngest Georgina Dove Freemantle was born 29 October 1867 in Hopetown.

They had twelve children together, and they lived in Grahamstown until after the birth of their fifth child in 1848. During this time, George had formed a partnership with Phillip Penny, but this was dissolved on 31 May1842.

In 1848, the family moved to the Somerset district and bought a farm called 'Pendry'. George continued to farm there for about two years, until they moved to Cradock and thereafter to Middelberg. It is also recorded that he was in Grahamstown on 15.October.1850 soon after the birth of his son, George, in Somerset East.

After the news of the discovery of the first diamond was confirmed, they moved to Hopetown, where their youngest child was born in 1867. Sometime later, they moved on again, towards Kimberley, where George was 'accidentally drowned in the Riet River, at the diggings.' His occupations are designated as farmer and mason. He was drowned on 10 May1878.

His widow, Elizabeth, remained living in Kimberley, and died in that town more than ten years later on 16.1.1889.

6. Thomas Freemantle was the youngest child of Richard Freemantle (1) and his second wife Sarah Kent. He was their only child to have been born in South Africa.
He was born in 1822 in Grahamstown shortly before his father was murdered.
He moved with his mother and siblings to Grahamstown after his father's death. When his family moved to Grahamstown they lived with Samuel.
 His mother remarried two years later and he moved with her and Eliza to their new home.
On 28 September 1858, Thomas Freemantle married Mary Pascoe in Port Frances; the service was lead by Rev. Peter Syrce.
However, unfortunately, she died seven months later, on 20 April 1859, she was 33 years old.
Thomas Freemantle died 16 September 1886 a widower, having never remarried. He was buried in the Methodist cemetery in Grahamstown.

Generation No. 3

7. William Freemantle was the only child of Richard Freemantle (2) and his first wife Patience Freemantle nee Ford. William was born 10 November in Grahamstown.

He was only three months old, when his mother died on 16.2.1828. His father, Richard (2), seems to have remained in the Grahamstown district until at least 1832, when he signed as witness to the marriage of his half-sister, Eliza to Thomas Derbyshire on 9.7.1832, but was in Port Elizabeth when he married his second wife, Elizabeth Anna (Hannah) Hall on 18.12.1837.

At that time, William would have been ten years old.

It is presumed that William Freemantle's marriage took place in about 1848, at the age of twenty-one, when he married Phyllis Pitt, (daughter of John Pitt and Sarah Pitt nee Roberts), in Burgersdorp.

On 3.7.1857, William Freemantle bought a plot of land in Burgersdorp (No: 148 - for eight hundred and fifty pounds). He was a farmer and a blacksmith and family tradition has it that he was so strong that he 'could lift an ox above his head!' Nevertheless, he was undoubtedly a man of considerable physical strength. That seems to have been the characteristic most remembered by those who knew him.

Phyllis and William had six children, all of which were born in Burgersdorp except one. Patience Anne (Annie) Freemantle was the Eldest born in 1850.

The second child Lois Emma Freemantle was born in 1852 in Queenstown. She was followed 2 years later by their first son William Roberts Freemantle born 29 September 1854, next came John Henry (Jack) Freemantle born 8 July 1856. Five years later came James Albert (Jimmy) Freemantle born 10 June 1861 and the youngest Alice Jane Freemantle was born the following year on 28 November 1862, she unfortunately died at a young age.

William Freemantle died on 19 December 1868, aged 41, in Burgersdorp. After William's death, Phyllis moved to the farm 'Broughton' near Molteno, owned by her son-in-law, Charles John Broster and daughter, Lois Emma. Phyllis Freemantle lived a further thirty years, dying on 18th.July, 1898 and she was buried in the cemetery at Burgersdorp, next to her husband's grave.

8. Ellen Anne Freemantle was the second child of Richard Freemantle (2) and the first of his second marriage to Elizabeth Hannah Hall. She was born on 5 August 1838 in Port Elizabeth. She married her first husband Henry Walker a soldier, who died in one on the frontier battles. Her married her second Husband, Dr Lamb and moved to England. She did not have any children. She died in England at a unknown date

9. Frances Elizabeth Freemantle was the third child of Richard Freemantle (2) and the second of his second marriage to Elizabeth Hannah Hall. Frances was born in 1840. She married a Mr. Pos.

Children of Frances Elizabeth Freemantle and Mr. Pos were:

    i   Richard Pos, born at the Little Fish River.

10. Robert John Freemantle was the fourth child of Richard Freemantle (2) and the third of his second marriage to Elizabeth Hannah Hall. He was born in 1841 in Port Elizabeth. Not much else is known about him.

11. George Richard Freemantle (2) was the fifth child of Richard Freemantle (2) and the fourth of his second marriage to Elizabeth Hannah Hall. He was born on 4 June 1843 in Port Elizabeth. He married Catherina Suzana Johanna Maria van den Berg in 1866 in Jansenville. She was born on 3 March 1844 in Holland.

George Richard Freemantle became a Park Manager and, although all their children were born in Jansenville, both he and his wife died in Uitenhage, he on 14.6.1918 and his wife during July 1926. They were buried next to one another in the Uitenhage cemetery their graves only being marked 'Father and Mother'. Many of their family were still living in that town in 1972 and some members are probably still to be found there. They had ten children.

12. John Freemantle was the eldest child of Samuel Freemantle and Sarah Freemantle nee Paxton. He was born on 10 January 1828 in Grahamstown. On 5 March 1856 he married in Grahamstown Harriet (Hannah) Miller, She was also born in Grahamstown on 21.3.1828. Her uncle, William Miller, was the founder of the Baptist Church in South Africa.

John Freemantle became a Prison Superintendent at Mount Frere and he died in that town, aged 84, on 12 September 1912; some thirty-nine years after the death of his wife Harriet on 18 May 1873. They had a very large family but it has not been possible to elicit details of all of them.

13. Lois Freemantle was the second child of Samuel Freemantle and Sarah Elizabeth Paxton. She was born on 7 December 1829 in Grahamstown; On 20 February 1849 at the age of 21, Lois Freemantle married Samuel Patten Impy, a shopkeeper in Fort Beaufort.

Samuel was born on 10 June 1828 at Whitby in Yorkshire. Samuel was a storekeeper in Fort Beaufort and on 23 July 1851, while traveling with four companions from Grahamstown on the way home to Fort Beaufort, he was ambushed on the Koonap Heights by rebel Hottentots and murdered.

Lois Impy nee Freemantle married her second husband Lennox James Bennett in 1853/4. He was born on 6 February 1818 in Cape Town.

Lennox James Bennett was a farmer in the McLear district where they both lived and, eventually, died within two months of each other. Lennox James Bennett died on 23 February 1884, aged 66 and Lois Bennett nee Freemantle died on 14 April 1884, aged 55. Samuel Impy was only about one years old when his father was killed and had been brought up within the family, as if he was his own, by his step-father, Lennox James Bennett.

14. Sarah Freemantle was the third child of Samuel Freemantle and Sarah Elizabeth Freemantle nee Paxton. She was born on 5 March 1832 in Grahamstown and when she was twenty, she married in Colesberg on 12 August 1852, Charles Benjamin Trollip. They moved to Vryburg and lived there for the duration of their married life.

15. Samuel Freemantle (2) was the fourth child of Samuel Freemantle and Sarah Elizabeth Freemantle nee Paxton. He was born in Grahamstown on 21 May 1833. He never married. He died in Grahamstown in 1855 at the age of 21 years

16. Emma Freemantle was the fifth child of Samuel Freemantle and Sarah Elizabeth Freemantle nee Paxton. She was born on 12 April 1835 in Grahamstown and she married in 1861, to Casper Henry Hartley. He was born on 6 March 1836 in the Tarka District. Casper became a printer and publisher in Kimberley and there were 13 children of this marriage. He died aged 69 years and 2 months on 23 May 1905 in Kimberley and his widow lived a further five years, dying aged 75 years on 20 September 1910 at the home of their son, Lennox Hartley, in Kimberley.

17. Charles (Charlie) Freemantle was the sixth child of Samuel Freemantle and Sarah Elizabeth Freemantle nee Paxton. He was born on 28 May 1837 in Grahamstown and spent his childhood there. In Cradock on 27 August 1878 he married Rachel McDonald, Rachel McDonald was born on 8.12.1850 in Winterberg, Cape. Charles Freemantle and Rachel had four children and he was a painter. He died in Cradock on 18 September 1906 and his widow lived until 23 June 1930, when she died in Johannesburg.

18. Harriet Freemantle was the seventh child of Samuel Freemantle and Sarah Elizabeth Freemantle nee Paxton. She was born on 18 May 1840 in Grahamstown. She was married on 4 January 1860 in Queenstown to Reuben Goulding. Reuben was also born in Grahamstown, on 25 September 1836 and he became a farmer at Bowker Park.

Eventually, Harriet and Reuben moved to the Witwatersrand and he died in Klerksdorp on 26 October 1896. Harriet Goulding died in 1902 in Johannesburg. There were nine children of her marriage to Reuben.

19. Elizabeth Freemantle was the eighth child Samuel Freemantle and Sarah Elizabeth Freemantle nee Paxton. She was born in Grahamstown on 13 May 1842.

On 28 March 1870, aged twenty-eight, she married in Cradock Jeremiah Woodland. He **was** an auctioneer and a general dealer in Cradock and there were four children of this marriage.

He died on 4 April 1888 at his own residence in Cradock, aged 48 years. The date and whereabouts of the death of Elizabeth Woodland nee Freemantle has not yet been traced, but she signed his death certificate, so it must have been after 1888.

20. Jesse William Freemantle was the ninth child of Samuel Freemantle and Sarah Elizabeth Freemantle nee Paxton. He was born in the Border Area of Albany on 1 April 1844. Jesse William Freemantle became a trader and. later, a farmer at Tarkastad in the eastern Cape Province. He was married in Tarkastad by the Rev. H. H. Dugmore on 27 March 1867 to Fanny Elizabeth Paxton, of Grahamstown, his mother's niece.

Fanny Elizabeth Paxton was born on 28.7.1842 in Grahamstown. There were eight children of the marriage, the first being born in Queenstown in 1868 and the second in Tarkastad in 1870. By 1879 they were living in the Transkei, probably at Umtata. Jesse died on 1 March 1924 at Queenstown, but the date and place of his wife's death have not been traced.

21. Jonathon Freemantle was the tenth child of Samuel Freemantle and Sarah Elizabeth Freemantle nee Paxton. He was born in 1847 and he died young.

22. Marianne Freemantle was the firstborn child of George Freemantle and Elizabeth Ann Stillwell. She was born in March 1841 in Grahamstown but she died six weeks later on 2 June 1841 in Grahamstown and was buried in the Methodist cemetery in Grahamstown.

23. Louisa Ann Freemantle was the second child of George Freemantle and Elizabeth Ann Stillwell. She was born in Grahamstown on 11 February 1842. She grew up as the eldest in the family after the death of the first born at six weeks of age. Her parents with their children, left Grahamstown when she was six years of age, in 1848 and moved to the Somerset district where her father farmed for a couple of years until they moved to Cradock in 1850 and then to Middleburg by 1853, by which time she was eleven.

When she was sixteen years old she married John Thornton Zachariah Fincham on 14 September 1858 in Middelburg. John was born on 6 June 1836 in Graff Reinet and he was a farmer and General Merchant. There were 12 children of this marriage and he died in Grahamstown on 13 March 1898. Louisa lived less than nine months after his death; also dying in Grahamstown on 1 December 1898; both at Rutherglen Cottage.

24. Mary Freemantle was the third child of George Freemantle and Elizabeth Ann Stillwell. She was born on 11 June 1844 in Grahamstown; she died six weeks later on 23 July 1844 in Grahamstown.

25. Sarah Elizabeth Freemantle was the fourth child of George Freemantle and Elizabeth Ann Stillwell. Two of her sisters died as infants, she grew up as the second oldest in the family. She was born on 29 March 1846 in Grahamstown. Two years later her parents left Grahamstown and moved to the Somerset district, where her father farmed for a couple of years, then just after the birth of her only brother in 1850, the family moved to Cradock, where another sister was born. When she was twelve they moved again, this time to Middelburg in the Cape. When she was 18 years old she married Christiaan Abraham van de Linde, on 12 September 1864 in Hanover in the Cape.

26. Harriet Martha Freemantle was the fifth child of George Freemantle and Elizabeth Ann Stillwel, but as two of her sisters had died as infants, she grew up as the third daughter of the family. She was born in Grahamstown on 16 September 1848 and her parents moved to the Somerset district while she was still an infant.

Her brother George was born there, but he too died, just before his third birthday, so that it was only her parents and the three girls who moved to Cradock sometime before 1852, when a fourth little girl was born. On 12 November 1866, at the age of 18 Harriet married Ralph Cawood in Hanover in the Cape; she was his second wife. Ralph Cawood, a farmer, was widowed when his first wife Elizabeth Cawood nee Dobson died, leaving four young children. Ralph Cawood was born at Manley Flats on 9 December 1829. Harriet and Ralph had ten children. Ralph Cawood died at Herbert, Vlakfontein, (Papkruil) , his own residence, on 22 April 1895. He left three farms and stock at his death, aged 65 years and 4 months.

27. George Richard Freemantle was the sixth child of George Freemantle and Elizabeth Ann Stillwell. He was born on 14 September 1850 in Somerset East and he died two months before his third birthday on 18 July 1853 in Middelburg

.

28. Emily Lois Freemantle was the seventh child of George Freemantle and Elizabeth Ann Stillwell. She had three older sisters, plus two who had died young and her brother, George Richard who was born about two years before she was, but died when she was nine months old. She was born on 23 October 1852 in Cradock. On 18 May 1870, aged 18, she married in Hopetown, David Sapsford. David was born in 1848. There were eleven children of this marriage.

29. Caroline Emma Freemantle was the eighth child of George Freemantle and Elizabeth Ann Stillwell. She was born on 5 November 1855 in Middelburg in the Cape. She died a spinster on 2 October 1944 in Cape Town.

30. Edith Cecilia Freemantle was the ninth child of George Freemantle and Elizabeth Ann Stillwell. She was born on 18 August 1858 in Middelburg in the Cape and she died there a month later in September 1858.

31. Edith Ann Freemantle was the tenth child of George Freemantle and Elizabeth Ann Stillwell, but at the time of her birth there were only five other sisters alive as three sisters and the only boy in the family had died young.

She was born in Middelburg, Cape on 28 December 1860; she was only 14 years of age when her father was drowned in the Riet River, near the diggings near Kimberley. On 28 June 1881, at the age of 21, she was married in Kimberley to Septimus Penny.

Septimus was born on 3 October 1859 in Bedford in the Cape; He became a farmer and, later, worked at the Big Hole in Kimberley. There were 8 or 9 children of his marriage to Edith Ann Freemantle. He died on 21 April 1930 in Kroonstad, followed sixteen years later by Harriet his widow, on 2 November 1946, also in Kroonstad.

32. Maud (Martha) Eliza Freemantle was the eleventh child of George Freemantle and Elizabeth Ann Stillwell. She was born on 14 May 1864 in Middelburg in the Cape. She married Herbert Brown on the 14 April 1908 in Vryburg; they had no children. She died on 1 August 1950 in Cape Town.

33.   Georgina Dove Freemantle was the twelfth and youngest child of George Freemantle and Elizabeth Ann Stillwell. She was born on 29 October 1867 in Hopetown in the Cape, she married **Louis P. Boshoff** on 10 October 1893 in Vryburg, and they had 5 children. Georgina died on 21 March 1939.

Generation No. 4

34. Patience Anne (Annie) Freemantle was the eldest daughter of William Freemantle and Phyllis Freemantle (nee Pitt). She was born Burgersdorp in 1850. She remained in that town her entire life. She never married and was a well-known music teacher, still remembered in the 1970's by some of the older residents and the children who were her pupils. She live with her mother until here mother died in a house opposite the Dopper Church, where she then lived on her own until her death in 1912.

35. Lois Emma Freemantle was the second child of William Freemantle and Phyllis Freemantle (nee Pitt). She was born on 16 October 1852 in Burgersdorp, on 18 November 1873; at the age of 21 she married Charles John Broster. He was a farmer and a merchant, born 9 May 1842 in Fort Beaufort, and died on 27 May 1926 on the farm 'Broughton' near Molteno.

36. William Roberts Freemantle was the third child of William Freemantle and Phyllis Freemantle (nee Pitt). He was born on 29 September 1854 in Burgersdorp and baptised on 24 October 1854, in the Methodist Church. He was educated at the Albert Academy in Burgersdorp.

He undertook transport riding by ox wagon to the early Kimberley diggings. On 8 October 1885, aged 31, he married in Burgersdorp, Martha Margaretha Joubert.

At the time of their wedding, she was twenty-one years old. Martha was born in Burgersdorp on 18 October 1863.

William and Margaretha Freemantle remained in Burgersdorp until about 1897, when they moved to Cala. By then five children had been born of this marriage, although one son, Allen, who was born in Burgersdorp on 29th.November, 1894, died at about four years of age.

They had eight children in all. But, unfortunately, the marriage was not a very happy one and eventually William parted from the family; their eldest son, Arthur remained with his grandparents at their farm 'Rietfontein' and continued his schooling in Burgersdorp, the elder daughters married and Eric and the younger ones remained with their mother. The family came to Johannesburg in 1904, where they stayed mostly in the centre of the town, William, settled in Potchefstroom and, later lived in Kroonstad, in both towns practicing as an auctioneer and agent.

William Roberts Freemantle died on 2nd.August, 1923 at the farm 'Welgenoit' in the district of Marico, Transvaal, aged 65 and Margaretha Freemantle died on 28th.December, 1932 in Pretoria at the home of her daughter, May Cormack.

37. John Henry (Jack) Freemantle was the fourth child of William Freemantle and Phyllis Freemantle (nee Pitt). He was born on the 8 July 1856 in Burgersdorp. He was baptised on 28 September 1856 in the methodist Church. On 3 June 1981 he married Lizzie Bibbey, in Burgersdorp. Lizzie was born 26 December 1887 in Cheshire, England. He was a clerk and a storekeeper and they had only one child, a son called Charles Henry Freemantle. John Henry Freemantle died in 1907 in Burgersdorp and his wife lived until 1957, when she died in East London. As a widow she was remarried, on 28.5.1908 in Burgersdorp, to Ernest James Horne.

38. James Albert (Jimmy) Freemantle was the fifth child of William Freemantle and Phyllis Freemantle (nee Pitt.) He was born in Burgersdorp on 10 June 1861 and was baptised at the Methodist Church there, at the same ceremony as his younger sister, Alice Jane Freemantle, on 29 December1862. He became a bookkeeper and married his first wife was Jessica Annie Jones, born in May 1868. On 5 October 1889 she died in Doornfontein, Johannesburg, aged 21 years and 5 months, at the birth of their first child, who also did not survive.

James Albert Freemantle married, his second wife on 14 April 1897 Clara Agnes Miles, who was born on 16 August 1861 and they had only one child, a daughter Carine Freemantle. She was born on 17.3.1898 in Dordrecht. When James Albert Freemantle died in Dordrecht 0n 30.9.1917, his widow and daughter remained on, living in that town and on 20.7.1921, Clara Agnes Freemantle nee Miles died on 22.6.1930

39. ? Freemantle (nee Pitt.). She was born on 28 November 1862 in Burgersdorp and she died at a young age.

40. Susana Catherina Freemantle was the first-born child of George Richard Freemantle (1) and Catherina Suzana Johanna Maria van den Berg. She was born on 22 January 1868 in Jansenville, She died as an infant on 21 November 1869 in Jansenville and was baptised the following day.

41. Sarah Freemantle was the second child of George Richard Freemantle (1) and Catherina Suzana Johanna Maria van den Berg. She was born on 22 June 1869 in Jansenville. Sarah married Johannes Nel in June 1885 in Uitenhage. She died on 25 April 1955 in Uitenhage.

42. Johanna Francina Maria Charlotte Freemantle was the third child of George Richard Freemantle (1) and Catherina Suzana Johanna Maria van den Berg. She was born in Jansenville in 1871, Her first husband was a Mr. Grobler and she married her 2nd husband Mr. Fouche on 12 April 1915, he was 50 years old and a farmer. She died on 1 June 1946.

43. Catherina Joanna Maria Freemantle was the fourth child of George Richard Freemantle (1) and Catherina Suzana Johanna Maria van den Berg. She was born on 11 July 1872 in Jansenville. Catherina married George William Edward Bubb on 20 February 1896 in Uitenhage. William worked for the railways what he did is unknown. She died 20 February 1896 in Uitenhage.

44. Jacobus Wilhelmus Freemantle (1st) was the fifth child of George Richard Freemantle (1) and Catherina Suzana Johanna Maria van den Berg. b. 7 July 1875 in Jansenville. When he was young he was a soldier, then he became a Machinist, joined the South African Railways as a policeman and, later, was a farmer.
He married his 1st wife Adrianna Johanna van Loggenberg on 20 May 1903 in Uitenhage. Adrianna was born on 17 September 1884 and confirmed in the Dutch Reformed Church on 28 April 1903 in Uitenhage. She died there in 1911. They had three children.

Jacobus married his 2nd wife Susanna Christina Adriana Knoetze on 21 October 1912 in Uitenhage and there were eleven children of this second marriage. He died on 23 January 1945 in Kirkwood.

45. Ellen Johanna Freemantle who was the sixth child of George Richard Freemantle and Catherina Suzana Johanna Maria van den Berg. Ellen was born on 29.6.1877 in Jansenville and was married in Uitenhage on 26.12.1894 to Edward James Bubb, who was a clerk and a miner. Edward was born on 16th May 1841 in Uitenhage, Cape, South Africa.

46. George Richard Freemantle [3rd] who was the seventh child of George Richard Freemantle and Catherina Suzana Johanna Maria van den Berg. George was born on 7 November 1879 in Jansenville and he became a Boiler Maker in the South African Railways. He married Christine (Polly) Claasen van Loggenberg in about 1913. She was born on 10.6.1892 in Vanderbyl Park, Transvaal. They had eight children. He died on 30.7.1928 in Uitenhage and she married (2nd) John Cecil Morris by whom she had two children.

47. Johannes Jacobus Francois Freemantle was the eighth child of George Richard Freemantle (1) and Christina (Polly) Claasen Freemantle nee van Loggenberg. He was born on 21 October 1881 in Jansenville. He became a Transport Rider. Johannes was married in Uitenhage on 24 September 1906 to Catherina A, Vermaak and died after 3 months in Uitenhage, on 6 January 1907. She remarried in 1908 Charles C. Phillipson (aged 25, a farmer).

48. Elizabeth Fracina Freemantle was the ninth child of George Richard Freemantle (1) and Christina (Polly) Claasen Freemantle nee van Loggenberg. She was born on 26 October 1883 in Jansenville and she died on 15.6.1963 in Uitenhage. She married Thomas Henry Bubb on 5.2.1900 in Uitenhage. He was a clerk in the railways.

49. Sibella Elizabeth Freemantle was the tenth child of George Richard Freemantle (1) and Christina (Polly) Claasen Freemantle nee van Loggenberg. She was born on 25 October 1885 in Jansenville, baptized on 11 April 1886 and married Alfred Herbert Bubb in 1903/4.
He was a Moulder on the South African Railways. She died 28.7.1913 in Uitenhage.

50. Henry John Freemantle was the first-born child of John Freemantle and Harriet (Hannah) Miller. Henry was born 29 December 1856 and he died at the age 24 on 13 September 1880. It is not known if he married and had children.

51. Louisa Emma Freemantle was the second child of John Freemantle and Harriet (Hannah) Miller. She was born on 16 August 1858 and she died at 10 months old on 15 April 1859.

52. Frederick Charles Freemantle was the third child of John Freemantle and Harriet (Hannah) Miller. He was born on 18 July 1859 He became a trader and a farmer. He never married. He died in 1945 in Matatiele.

53. Samuel Walter Freemantle was the fourth child of John Freemantle and Harriet (Hannah) Miller. He was born on 1 February 1861 and he married Barbara Margaretha Susahanna Hofmeyr.
She was born on 4.7.1875 and died on 20.4.1960, twenty-two years after her husband, Samuel, who died on 9.1.1938 at Mount Frere, which is where they lived and where their four children were born..

54. Alfred Ellington Freemantle was the fifth child of John Freemantle and Harriet (Hannah) Miller. He was born on 29 April 1862 in Queenstown. He became a prospector. He married **Evelyn** Sophia Meek; he died on 12 October 1925. He had no children.

55. George Arthur Freemantle was the sixth child of John Freemantle and Harriet (Hannah) Miller. He was born 29 October 1863, his 1st wife was a Miss Molly ? and he married his 2nd wife Amalia Amelia Augusta Schaeffer in 1888; she was a widow with three children. He died on 17 November 1931 at Mount Frere, but was buried at Umtata.

Children of George Arthur Freemantle and Amalia Amelia Augusta Schaeffer were:
    i   **Donavan Freemantle,** died young.

56. Harriet Eliza Freemantle was the eighth child of John Freemantle and Harriet (Hannah) Miller. She was born on 25 July 1866, She married a Mr. McCabe, but had no children. She died on 26 May 1926.

57. Anna Maria Freemantle was the tenth child of John Freemantle and Harriet (Hannah) Miller. She was born on 16 July 1868; she married in Livingston to a Mr. Willmer. They were living in Zambia in the 1970's. Unknown if they had children.

58 Lennox James Freemantle was the eleventh child of John Freemantle and Harriet (Hannah) Miller. She was born on 16 October 1870, died on the 23 of an unknown month and year.

59. Annie Freemantle was the thirteenth child of John Freemantle and Harriet (Hannah) Miller. She married a Mr. Werener. They had no children.

60. Walter Freemantle was the fourteenth child of John Freemantle and Harriet (Hannah) Miller. not much else is know about him.

61. Robert Freemantle was the fifteenth child of John Freemantle and Harriet (Hannah) Miller. He married Ethna Mildred.

62. Ethel Millicent Freemantle was the eldest child of Charles Freemantle and Rachel McDonald. She was born on 28 September 1881 in Cradock. She married at the age of 22 years to Frederick Charles Smith. Frederick was born in 1877 in England; he was a telegraphist. She died at the age of 90 on 10 October 1971.

63. Samuel Bertram Freemantle was the second child of Charles Freemantle and Rachel McDonald. He was born on 21 January 1884 in Cradock. He married Florence Gertrude Hutchings on the 7 August 1912 in Jo-burg. Florence was born on the 8 August 1884 in Zoutpansberg, Tvl. Samuel died on 4 December 1960 in Pietermaritzburg, Natal. Florence died on 31 October 1966 in Durban.

64. Ernest John Freemantle was the third child of Charles Freemantle and Rachel McDonald. He was born on 9 September 1988 in Pretoria. He was a Farmer and a Mine Swelterer. He married Mary Jane Hester Collen on 9 September 1913 in Vryburg. Mary was born on 1 September 1981 in Barkley West in the Cape. Ernest died in 1972 in Bedfordview in the Tvl.

65 . Norman McDonald Freemantle was the fourth child of Charles Freemantle and Rachel McDonald. He was born on the 11 August 1892, he married Beatrice Chick, and they had no children. On Norman's 78th Birthday on 11 August 1970, Normon and Beatrice died tragically together on the South Coast of Natal; they were buried in the same grave at Port Shepstone.

66. Amy Millicent Freemantle was the eldest child of Jesse William Freemantle and Fanny Elizabeth Paxton. She was born on 26 June 1868 in Queenstown; she married Albert Sobey. She died in 1953 in Johannesburg.

67. Percy William Freemantle was the second child of Jesse William Freemantle and Fanny Elizabeth Paxton. He was born on 24 March 1870 Tarkastad. He married Ada Blance Cowen in 1892 in Mount Frere in Transkei. He died in 1960 in Matatiele.

68. Charles White Freemantle was the third child of Jesse William Freemantle and Fanny Elizabeth Paxton. He was born on 2 October 1872 in Cradock. He died young.

69. Minnie Lois Freemantle was the fourth child of Jesse William Freemantle and Fanny Elizabeth Paxton. She was born on 25 December 1874 in Cradock. She died young.

70. Clifford Bailey Freemantle was the fifth child of Jesse William Freemantle and Fanny Elizabeth Paxton. He was born on 28 June 1876 in Umtata, Transkei. He died in 1889 at the age of 13 years in Umtata.

71. Oliver Woodland Freemantle was the sixth child of Jesse William Freemantle and Fanny Elizabeth Paxton. He was born on 18 February 1879 in Transkei.

He married his first wife Muriel Selina Goldsmith on 25 September 1907 in Fort Beaufort; Muriel was born in 1882. They got divorced on 5 November 1920, after 13 years of marriage; they had 1 child.

He married (a month later) his second wife Dorothy Frances Mates, on 9 December 1920 in Wynberg in Cape Town. Dorothy was born on 26 August 1893 in Arendal, Sussex in England.

Oliver died on 18 January 1949 in Cape Town. Dorothy died 10 years later on 18 January 1949 in Cape Town.

Children of Oliver Woodland Freemantle and Muriel Selina Goldsmith were:

    i   **Theodore Eileen Muriel Freemantle** no details have been traced

Children of Oliver Woodland Freemantle and Dorothy Frances Mates were:

72. Walter Harry Paxton Freemantle was the seventh child of Jesse William Freemantle and Fanny Elizabeth Paxton. He was born on 27 March 1881 in Umtata, Transkei. He married his 1st wife Rose Wedderburn, but they divorced in 1918, they had no children. He married his 2nd wife Elsie Flowers who was born on 28 January 1887 in Theale England, she died on 30 May 1963 in Cape Town, 5 years after Walter who died on 2 June 1958 in Umtata, Transkei.

Children of Walter Harry Paxton Freemantle and Elsie Flowers were:

124 i   **Anthea (Wendy) Paxton Freemantle b.** 23 April 1926 Mount Ayliff
125 ii   **Myles Paxton Freemantle b.** 8 July 1930 Reading, England,
            d. 2001 Montagu, Cape

73. Katie May Freemantle was the eighth child of Jesse William Freemantle and Fanny Elizabeth Paxton. She was born on 19 November 1882 in Umtata, Transkei. She married George Gibbs had 5 children - the eldest was called May Gibbs.

Generation No. 5

74. Phyllis Ida Freemantle was the eldest child of William Roberts Freemantle and Martha Margaretha Freemantle nee Joubert. She was born on 18 September 1886 and baptised in the Methodist church there. Her parents lived in Burgersdorp until 1897, so it is probable that she received some schooling there.

Phyllis married her first husband Alec Powell in Johannesburg in 1908 or 1909. He was born and died in that city, but the dates are unknown at this time. He worked in a factory in Johannesburg and there were six children of this marriage, all born in Johannesburg.

Phyllis married her second husband William Newnham in Durban in 1951. He was born in England and died in Durban in 1968. He was a farmer. In 1972, Phyllis was residing at Jafta House, Prince Street, Durban and she died there in December 1973.

75. Ethal Margaret Freemantle was the second child of William Roberts Freemantle and Martha Margaretha Freemantle nee Joubert. She was born in Burgersdorp on 18th. September 1887 and her parents lived there until she was ten years old, then they moved to Cala.

In 1904 the family moved to Johannesburg. On 16 February 1910 she married Thomas (Tommie) Pike Goulding (son of Reuben Goulding and Harriet Goulding nee Freemantle) in Johannesburg. He was born on 28 December 1880 in Kimberley.

Ethel and Thomas had 3 sons and 2 daughters, the third child, Joy Kathleen Goulding, died at seven months old at Whites, in the Orange Free State, where they lived until 1924.

During the Depression they moved to Colenso and afterwards to Bramley, Jo-burg, where they lived for a number of years, and then moved to a farm called 'Aloepoort' in the Zastron district and close to the Basutuland border. Thomas Pike Goulding was a farmer and an engineer. He died on 8 August 1957 at 'Aloepoort'. Ethel, moved to Ladysmith to be near her daughter, Margaret and family, and she died there on 30th.September, 1967.

The children of Thomas Pike Goulding and Ethel Margaret Freemantle were:

    i   **Allan Kenneth Goulding** b. 19 December 1910 in Jo-burg, m. Gilda Leonie Bosenberg on 15 December 1939 in Cape Town , he died 17 February 1983 in Frere Hospital. They had 3 children: Kenneth Christian Goulding, Michael Thomas Goulding, Allan Merrick Goulding.

76. Lois May Freemantle was the third child of William Roberts Freemantle and Margaretha Freemantle nee Joubert. She was born in Burgersdorp on 8 November 1889. Lois May Freemantle trained as a nurse.

In 1919 she married Jack Cormack in Jo-burg. Jack was born in Burgersdorp in 1880; he died in Bloemfontein in 1943.

Although May and Jack's family started with three sets of twins, during the time they were living in Cape Town, they all died very young, as infants.

Then a single child was born, their only remaining child, Margaret Cormack, Her parents separated and were divorced sometime before World War II.

May continued nursing and became a matron of a number of hospitals or nursing homes.

In July 1944, she married again, to a retired shopkeeper from Ficksburg, who was farming near Bethlehem called George Bishop. He was a widower, having previously been married to Louisa van Soelen (who died in 1934), with whom he had 5 sons and one daughter; all of whom were living in the Bethlehem-Ficksburg area in the 1970's. George Bishop died only a few years after this marriage and there was no issue of this union. May died in Durban in 1959/60.

Children of Lois May Freemantle and Jack Cormack.

   i   **Margaret Cormack** b. 14 December 1924 in Cape Town, m. Michael Hathorn on 17th April, 1943 in Jo-burg They had four children.

77. Arthur William James Freemantle was the fourth child of William Roberts Freemantle and Martha Margaretha Freemantle nee Joubert. He was born in Burgersdorp on 8 October 1890 and was baptised in the Methodist Church there on 21 December 1890.

When his parents moved to Cala in 1897, Arthur remained with his grandparents, Jotham and Martha M.J.Joubert, at their farm 'Rietfontein' just outside Burgersdorp, He was confirmed in the Dutch Reformed Church in Burgersdorp, aged 16, in 1907.

He started to work as young man with the Victoria Falls and Transvaal Power Company (which later became ESCOM) and at first was mainly employed on the Witwatersrand and later at Witbank, where he met Frances Letty.

In the 1914-18 War he served first in South West Africa with the Imperial Light Horse and at the end of hostilities there, joined Major Miller's contingent and went to England to join the R.A.F. (R.F.C.). He had just got his commission as a pilot when the war came to an end.

On 11 June 1921 in Pretoria, he married Frances Josephine Letty. She was born on 27 January 1893; they had 3 children.

In the Second World War, Arthur served as a Captain in the South African Air Force and went up north to the Western Desert.

When Arthur retired, they purchased a farm near Vereeniging and lived there for some years. Frances Josephine Freemantle died in Durban on 17th. March, 1961 and Arthur William James Freemantle died in Bramley, Johannesburg on 3rd.September, 1970, 'where he had been for some months'.

Children of Arthur William James Freemantle and Frances Josephine Letty were:

126 i   **Elinda Lois Freemantle** b. 8 January 1923 in Zeerust, m. John Edgar Dale (Bill) Bramwell on 5 July 1947 in Jo-burg. He was born 3 September 1920 in Vryheid, Natal.

127ii   **Alric Joubert Freemantle** b. 3 June 1924 in Randfontein, m. Patricia Bennett 3 March 1951 in Pretoria. She was born on 21 December 1925 in East London.

128iii   **Arthur Walter (Bob) Freemantle** b. 27 November 1928 in Milnerton, Cape, m. 1st wife Diedreka Venemans in Jo-burg on 4 July 1953. They divorced in 1978.

78. Allen Freemantle was the fifth child of William Roberts Freemantle and Martha Margaretha Freemantle nee Joubert. He was born on 29 November 1894 in Burgersdorp, he died when he was only 4 years old.

79. Eric Freemantle was the sixth child of William Roberts Freemantle and Martha Margaretha Freemantle nee Joubert. He was born 25 April 1896, in Burgersdorp and baptised in the Methodist Church there on 3rd.August, 1896.

He attended school until the age of thirteen. In 1914 at the outbreak of WW1 he joined the third African Infantry.

On 3 November 1920 he married his first wife, Phyllis Howard at St. Patrick's Church in Jo-burg. Phyllis was born in Cala, Cape, on 1st September 1897.
Phyllis died on Sunday, 16th December 1957 at her home in Dunked. Her ashes are in the Garden of Remembrance in Johannesburg.

Eric was married a second time, in about 1958, to Alice Letty nee Tidmarsh; Alice was previously married to Marcus Letty. From which she had four children; Leonie, Christine, Edwin, and a late child, Marcus Eric but who, after her second marriage, was adopted by E.F. and legally acquired the name of his adoptive parent, Eric Freemantle.

Eric died on 7 December 1972. Alice died on Sunday, 24th.June, 2001.

80. Letitia (Jill) Freemantle was the seventh child of William Roberts Freemantle and Martha Margaretha Freemantle nee Joubert. She was born on 22 February 1898 in Cala in the Cape. On 21 April 1921 Letitia (Jill) Freemantle married Thornton Archer in Johannesburg. He was born on 4 December 1892 in Molteno.

Thornton was a farmer and also a mine production manager. He died on 16.10.1964 in Grahamstown. Soon after they were married, Jill started a correspondence school for the children of farmers, or those living in rural areas who had difficulty in attending regular primary or pre-primary schools.
This was the first enterprise of this kind in South Africa and proved to be remarkably successful, though it required considerable work on her part.
In later life they moved to the Grahamstown area, living as mentioned, for some years in Bathurst, where in 1970, Jill was made mayor of that town. Some time after Thornton's death, Jill moved to the Rustenberg district, living on a small holding not far from the home of her daughter, Patricia and her family. She eventually died there on 5.2.1979, aged 81.

81. Ronald Roberts Freemantle, was the eighth and youngest child of William Roberts Freemantle and Martha Margaretha Freemantle nee Joubert. He was born in Indwe on 3rd.May, 1900 and baptised in the Presbyterian Church there. Ronald Roberts Freemantle was married in Johannesburg on 4 August 1928 in the Yeoville Catholic Church, to Constance Pauline Harrison, the daughter of George Washington Harrison and Pauline Harrison nee Emmerich.

Constance (Connie) was born in Johannesburg on 13th. April, 1904 and baptised in the Roman Catholic Church there. During 1916/1917 Ronald served in the German East African forces with the South African Service Corps. - Mechanical Transport - and drove a car on the narrow gauge railway between Kilwa and Lundi.

He spent a considerable time in hospital suffering from sunstroke and malaria.
In 1948, owing to financial problems, Ronald left the Stock Exchange one of many of his jobs and they went farming in the Lydenberg district. With the assistance of their three sons, Con and Ron farmed there for about 15 years and then returned to Johannesburg, where Ron went to work for the firm, Max Pollak & Freemantle. He retired in 1969.

Their son, Joseph (Joe) had built onto his home in Bryanston a 'granny-flat' in which his parents lived until their deaths. Ronald died on 20 May 1981 and Constance died during a visit to the home of her son, Paul, in Kloof, Natal, on 21 April 1988.

82. Charles Henry Freemantle b. 9 February 1894 in Burgersdorp, d. 26 May 1963 in Stutterheim. He was a farmer.
He married his 1st wife Nellie Florence Maud Rouse on 7 April 1919 in Komgha.
She was born on 26 March 1899 in McLear and she died on 4September 1962 in Queenstown. They were divorced in 1949 and he married his 2nd wife Elizabeth Barnard on 8 August 1951 in Aliwal North. There were no children from the second marriage.

Children of Charles Henry Freemantle and Nellie Florence Maud Rouse were:

137 **i** **Kenneth Freemantle** b. 9 January 1920 in Bloemfontein, m. Barbara Trenbath on 14 July 1945.

83. Carine Freemantle was the only child of James Albert Freemantle and Clara Agnes Miles. She was born on 17 March 1898 in Dordrecht, she married Eric Ivan Larter on 20 July 1921. She died on 22 April 1944 in Dalkeith', Molteno, had 3 children.

84. George Richard Freemantle (2nd) was the eldest Child of Wilhelmus Freemantle and Adrianna Johanna van Loggenberg. He was born in 1904 in Uitenhage and married there on 29 May 1930 to Emily Matilda Shaw. She was born in the Stockenstroom district on 23 January 1905 and they had four children:

Children of George Richard Freemantle (2nd) and Emily Matilda Shaw were:

85. Christina Freemantle was the second child of Wilhelmus Freemantle and Adrianna Johanna van Loggenberg. She was born on 19 October 1906 in Uitenhage. She got married at the age of 33 years to Jan Jacobus Stephanus du Toit on 15 July 1939. She died 6 years later in Kirkwood on 25 October 1945 at the birth of her first child.

Children of Christina Freemantle and Jan Jacobus S. du Toit were:

86. Catherina Sarah Johanna Maria Freemantle was the third child of Wilhelmus Freemantle and Adrianna Johanna van Loggenberg. She was born on 24 March 1909 in Uitenhage. She died in 1928 of tuberculosis; she was not married.

87. Susannah Christina Freemantle was the fourth child of Jacobus Wilhelmus Freemantle and the first of his 2nd marriage to Susanna Christina Adrianna Knoetze. She was born on 7 August 1913 in Uitenhage, she married J.S. Fourie, a builder.

88. Sarah Freemantle was the second child, of the second marriage of Jacobus Wilhelmus Freemantle and Susanna Christina Adrianna Knoetze. She was born on 4 November 1914 in Uitenhage and she married Mathew Calitz the Manager of the Citrus Co-Op in Patensie and they lived in Jeffreys Bay.

89. Jacobalina Wilhelmina Freemantle was the third child of the second marriage of Jacobus Wilhelmus Freemantle and Susanna Christina Adrianna Knoetze. She was born on 4 February 1916 in Uitenhage and married Christiaaan du Toit, a farmer at Magogeng.

90. Jacobus Wilhelmus Freemantle (2nd), was the fourth child of the second marriage of Jacobus Wilhelmus Freemantle and Susanna Christina Adrianna Knoetze. He was born on 3 December 1918 in Uitenhage. He was a Police W.O. in Harrismith and he married Sophia de Villiers.

91. Adriaan Frederick Freemantle was the fifth child of the second marriage of Jacobus Wilhelmus Freemantle and Susanna Christina Adrianna Knoetze. He was born on 15 October 1920 in Uitenhage. He died in Pretoria on 9 July 1984.

He married in Pretoria on 11 May 1946 Wilhelmina Lodervika Coetzee. She was born on 17 December 1920. They had five children:

92. Johannes Jacobus (John) Freemantle was the sixth child of the second marriage of Jacobus Wilhelmus Freemantle and Susanna Christina Adrianna Knoetze. He was born on 28 August 1922 in Uitenhage.

He married at the age of 23 years on 1 September 1945, to Dorothy May Kroezen. May was born in Cape Town on 11 of October 1924.
He works for the South African Railways as a Mechanical Engineer. They lived in Noordhoek in the Cape, John died on 26 July 2000 in Cape Town. And they had four children:

> **93. Maria Petronella Freemantle** was the seventh child of the second marriage of Jacobus Wilhelmus Freemantle and Susanna Christina Adrianna Knoetze. She was (m?) on 29 September 1924 in Uitenhage. Maria married **Wilhelm** Landman, who worked for the South African Railways in Durban.

94. Robert Pienaar Freemantle was the eighth child of the second marriage of Jacobus Wilhelmus Freemantle and Susanna Christina Adrianna Knoetze. He was born on 26 July 1926 in Uitenhage. He became Senior Revenue Inspector in Cradock and he married Johanna Maria (Joan) Kroezen. She was born on 14 August 1929 in Cape Town and they had four children:

95. Stanley Freemantle the ninth child of the second marriage of Jacobus Wilhelmus Freemantle and Susanna Christina Adrianna Knoetze. He was born on 30 August 1928 in Uitenhage and died in April 1965. He was unmarried.

96. Leslie Freemantle was the tenth child of the second marriage of Jacobus Wilhelmus Freemantle and Susanna Christina Adrianna Knoetze. He was born on 12 February 1932 in Uitenhage and he married in Bloemfontein on 4 June 1957 Daline Johanna van Lingen. Daline was born on 5 November 1937 in Petrusburg, O.F.S. and they had four children:

97. Lynel Freemantle was the eleventh child of the second marriage of Jacobus Wilhelmus Freemantle and Susanna Christina Adrianna Knoetze. Lynel was born on 20 May 1934 in Kirkwood and he married in Durban on 27 July 1957 at the age of 23 years, Susanna Jakoba Petronella Koster. Susanna was born on 27 July 1939. Lynel became a carpenter and joiner and General Foreman of Constructions, working for Bridge and Construction Engineers. They had six children:

98. George Richard Freemantle (5th), was the eldest child of George Richard Freemantle (3rd) and Christine (Polly) Claasen van Loggenberg. He was born on 20 August 1914 in Uitenhage and died two weeks later on 8 September 1914 in Uitenhage.

99. Gideon Christian Freemantle was the second child of George Richard Freemantle (3rd) and Christine (Polly) Claasen van Loggenberg. He was born on 23 September 1915 in Uitenhage. He became a Bottle Store Manager. He married Catherine Maria Botes. Catherine was born on 18 December 1924 in Pretoria and they had five children.

100. Richard George Freemantle who was the fourth child of George Richard Freemantle (3rd) and Christine (Polly) Claasen van Loggenberg. He was born after a daughter who died young. Richard was born on 31 October 1918 in Uitenhage. He became a wheel tester. He married Salomie Meyer, who was born in 1919 and died on 20 July 1975. They had no children.

101. Douglas Frederick Freemantle was the fifth child of George Richard Freemantle (3rd) and Christine (Polly) Claasen van Loggenberg. He was born in November 1920 in Uitenhage. He died at 11 months old on 1 October 1921 in Uitenhage.

102. Robert John Freemantle was the sixth child of George Richard Freemantle (3rd) and Christine (Polly) Claasen van Loggenberg. He was born on 3 August 1922 in Uitenhage and he became a salesman. He married his 1st wife Monica Dorothea Goosen in Bellville in the Cape on 16 July 1949. They were divorced on 1 August 1957. They had no children.

He married his 2nd wife Eliza Gertrude van der Merwe on 3 August 1957 in Pretoria and there were no children of this marriage either.

103. Annis Powry Freemantle was the seventh child of George Richard Freemantle (3rd) and Christine (Polly) Claasen van Loggenberg. He was born on 11 March 1924 in Uitenhage and he became a Charge man. Annis married Susannah Coetze, she was born on 10 February 1926 in Transvaal.
Children of Annis Powry Freemantle and Susannah Coetze were:

104. Raymond Charles Freemantle was the eighth child of George Richard Freemantle (3rd) and Christine (Polly) Claasen van Loggenberg. He was born in 1927 in Uitenhage and died 23 February 1928 in Uitenhage.

105. Fred Wilfred Freemantle was the eldest child of Samuel Walter Freemantle and Barbara M. S. Hofmeyr. Fred was born on 25 June 1909 and he was married in 1936 at Tsolo, Transkei to Emmerentia Bezuidenhout , who was born in Tsolo and they had seven children:

106. Clifford Walter Gordon Freemantle was the second child of Samuel Walter Freemantle and Barbara M. S. Hofmeyr. Clifford who was born on 5 February 1911 at Mount Frere and he became a mechanic. On 19 September 1938 he married Eileen Dorothy Cromhout, she was born on 13 November 1911 at Mount Frere and they had six children:

107. Ethna Mildred Freemantle was the third child of Samuel Walter Freemantle and Barbara M. S. Hofmeyr. She was born on 16 January 1912 at Mount Frere and she married there on 11 May 1934 Clarence Cromhout who was a trader. He was born on 1 December 1914 at Mount Frere and he died 10 July 1966 in Zululand.

108. Alfred Ellington Freemantle was the fourth child of Samuel Walter Freemantle and Barbara M. S. Hofmeyr. He was born 4 May 1914 at Mount Frere and he died in 1974 at Pietermaritzburg. He never married.

109. Edna Winifred Freemantle was the eldest child of Samuel Bertram Freemantle and Florence Gertrude Hutchings she was born on 30 July 1913 in Potchefstroom, Transvaal. Edna married at the age of 25 to William Earle MacIntyre on the 31 December 1938 in Johannesburg. William was a businessman and in Advertising, he was born on 27 April 1912 in Jo-burg. He died on 21 September 1959.

110. Bertram Stanley Freemantle was the second child of Samuel Bertram Freemantle and Florence Gertrude Hutchings. He was born on 15 July 1919 in Jo-berg. He married on 15 July 1940 in Jo-burg, Alicia Petronella (Helen) Rosebrook. Alicia was born on 29 December 1919 Johannesburg.

111. Cecil Reginald Freemantle was the third child of Samuel Bertram Freemantle and Florence Gertrude Hutchings. He was born on 6 April 1923 in Jo-berg. He was a S.A. Air Freight Official. He married Eva Duysel **in** 1945/6 in Durban, Natal. They eventually divorced 5 children:

112. Aubrey Lionel Freemantle was the fourth child of Samuel Bertram Freemantle and Florence Gertrude Hutchings. He grew up as the youngest because his two sisters born after him died young. He was born on 26 March 1927 in Potchefstroom, Tvl. He was a **Mining** Electrician. He got married in 1953 in Jo-burg to Heila Magdelina.

113. Thelma Freemantle was the fifth child of Samuel Bertram Freemantle and Florence Gertrude Hutchings. She was born on 6 August 1915 in Jo-burg; she died in her fifth year on 15 December 1920 in Jo-berg.

114. Doreen Freemantle was the sixth child of Samuel Bertram Freemantle and Florence Gertrude Hutchings. She was born on 16 July 1916 in Jo-burg. She died in her ninth year on 7 December 1925 in Potchefstroom.

115. Myrtle Freemantle was the eldest child of Ernest John Freemantle and Mary Jane Hester Collen. She was born on 21 May 1914. She married Ernest Edward Davey; they had 3 children. Myrtle died on 21 July 1943.

116. Phyllis Thora Freemantle was the second child of Ernest John Freemantle and Mary Jane Hester Collen, she was born on 6 October 1915. She married Redvers Williams and they had 3 children.

117. Stella Joy Freemantle was the third child of Ernest John Freemantle and Mary Jane Hester Collen. She was born on 18 April 1924; she married Leon Louw. They had 4 children.

118. Ronald Percy Cowen Freemantle was the eldest child of Percy William Freemantle and Ada Blanche Cowen. He was born on 8 March 1894 in Mount Frere, in the Transkei. He died while serving in the Royal Flying Corps in World War I in March 1917. He never married.

119. Lulu Dorothia Freemantle was the second child of Percy William Freemantle and Ada Blanche Cowen. She was born on 31 October 1897 in Mount Frere in the Transkei. She died in the 1980's in Matatiele, in East Griqualand; she never married.

Focus on John Mates Freemantle.

120. John Mates Freemantle was the eldest child of the second marriage of Oliver Woodland Freemantle and Dorothy Frances Mates. He was born on 12 March 1922 in Cape Town. At the age of 25 years he married **Doris Rona Boshoff** on 29 November 1947. They were married in Pinelands in the Cape and John Mates Freemantle became a stationmaster.

They spent many years in Northern Rhodesia.

Eventually John and Doris Freemantle emigrated from South Africa and went to Perth, Australia. There were five children of this marriage, as listed below.

Children of John Mates Freemantle and Doris Rona Boshoff were:

175 i   **June Frances Freemantle** b. 23. 6.1949 Cape Town
176 ii   **John Christian Freemantle** b. 20. 8.1951 Boksburg /Benoni
177 iii   **Rosemary Dawn Freemantle** b. 22. 7. 1953 Boksburg/Benoni
178 iv   **David Michael Freemantle** b. 14.11.1956 Que Que, Rhodesia
179 v   **Robin Errol Freemantle** b. 13. 4.1958 Que Que, Rhodesia

121. Douglas Paxton Freemantle was the third child of Oliver Woodland Freemantle and Dorothy Frances Mates second marriage. He was born on 9 November 1926 in Umtata in Transkei.

He was born 2 years after his second brother, who died shortly after birth. He was married in Observatory, Cape Town on 18 December 1948 to Patricia Magdeline Lotter; he was 22 years old.

He became an engineer and in the 1980's was working as Engineering Assistant at ESKOM.

Children of Douglas Paxton Freemantle and Patricia Magdeline Lotter were:

    i   **Ingrid Freemantle** b.29 September 1950 Bellville, Cape.

    ii   **Paul Douglas Freemantle** b.30 January 1953 Oranjemund, South West Africa

    iii   **Anthony Oliver Freemantle** b.11 December 1955 Oranjemund, South West Africa, d. 25 June 1985 Cape Town.

    iv   **Ronald Paxton Freemantle** b. 2 December 1959, Oranjemund, South West Africa.

122. Olive Frances Freemantle was the fourth child of Oliver Woodland Freemantle and Dorothy Frances Mates second marriage. Olive was born on 5 October 1928 in Britstown, in the Cape Province.

On 13 March 1954 in Lansdowne, Cape, at the age of 26 years, she married Donald Penfold. Donald became an electrical engineer and Olive Frances became a telegraphist.

Children of Olive Frances Freemantle and Donald Penfold were:

    i   **Stephen Wayne Penfold** b. 30 May 1955 Kitwe, Northern Rhodesia.
    ii   **Jennifer Lynn Penfold** b. 11 November 1958 Kitwe, Northern Rhodesia.
    iii **Denise Marcelle Penfold** b. 14 February 1961 Kitwe, Northern Rhodesia.

123. Neville Bailey Freemantle was the fifth child of Oliver Woodland Freemantle and Dorothy Frances Mates second marriage. Neville was born in Maclear on 5 July 1931. His occupation was that of Principal Works Inspector of Buildings. On 28 December 1957 Neville was married in the Dutch Reformed Church in Cape Town to Wilhelmina Johanna Kitshoff, Wilhelmina, was born in Stellenbosch on 13 May 1925.

Children of Neville Bailey Freemantle and Wilhelmina Johanna Kitshoff were:

i   **Erica Frances Freemantle** b. 23 October 1959 in Oranjemund, South West Africa, m. Mr. Loftus.
ii   **Michael Freemantle** b. 25 February 1962

124. Anthea (Wendy) Paxton Freemantle is the eldest child of Walter Harry Paxton Freemantle and Elsie Flowers. She was born on 23 April 1926 in Mount Ayliff. At 24 years she married John Arthur Vivian Ruck on 14 October 1950 in Cape Town. John was a business executive. He was born on 13 March 1923 in Port Elizabeth.

Children of Anthea (Wendy) Paxton Freemantle and John A V. Ruck were:
i   Peta Ruck b.28 November 1952 in Cape Town
ii   Myles Ruck b.7 June 1955 in Cape Town.

125. Myles Paxton Freemantle was the second child of Walter Harry Paxton Freemantle and Elsie Flowers. Myles was born on 8 July 1930 in Reading, England. He married his wife Gwenda and he became a barrister and practiced in Mateliele, East Griqualand for many years, then the family moved to Durban, Natal, where he continued his legal practice. He and his wife, Gwenda, retired to Montagu in the Cape and he died in Cape Town in June 2002.

Generation No. 6

126. Elinda Lois Freemantle eldest daughter of Arthur William James Freemantle and Frances Josephine Letty, born 8 January 1923 in Zeerust. She married John Edgar Dale (Bill) Bramwell on 5 July 1947 in Jo-burg. He was born 3 September 1920 in Vryheid, Natal, he was a Civil Engineer. They had five children.

127. Alric Joubert Freemantle, was the second child of Arthur William James Freemantle and Frances Josephine Letty, born on 3 June 1924 in Randfontein and he married Patricia Bennett on 3 March 1951 in Pretoria. She was born on 21 December 1925 in East London. They had 4 children:

Children of Alric Joubert Freemantle and Patricia Bennett were:
183 i   **Roderick John Freemantle** b. 12 October 1951 in Johannesburg, m. Elizabeth Goodwin.
    ii **Anthony Michael Freemantle** b. 5 January 1954, in Johannesburg.
    iii **Jeremy Arthur Freemantle** b. 14 December 1955, in Krugersdorp .
    iv **Patricia Ann Freemantle** b. 25 June 1960, in Johannesburg.
128. Arthur Walter (Bob) Freemantle was the third child of Arthur William James Freemantle and Frances Josephine Letty. He was born on 27.11.1928 in Milnerton, Cape and he became a Civil Engineer. He married his first wife Diedreka Venemans in Johannesburg on 4 July 1953. They divorced in 1978. m. 2nd wife Frances Josephine Letty.

Children of Arthur Walter (Bob) Freemantle and Frances Josephine Letty were:

184 i **Richard Joubert Freemantle** b. 19 August 1956, in Johannesburg, m. Sheila Guillard on 27 May 1979. She was born on 25 July 1952.

185ii **Diana Helen Freemantle** b.23 January 1959, in Johannesburg, m. Peter Weibel on 19September 1981. He was born on 10 June 1956, had a child Justin Paul Weibel.

186-iii **Barbara Joan Freemantle** b. 7 February 1964, in Johannesburg.

129. John Eric Freemantle, the eldest son of Eric Freemantle and Phyllis Freemantle nee Howard was born in Johannesburg on 15th April 1922.

On his twenty-second birthday, (15.4.1944) John married Marion Craig Smaling, by Rev. Pearson at St. Martin's-in-the-Veld, Rosebank. They had two daughters Jillian Leslie Freemantle in 1945 and Anne Terry Freemantle in 1947.

In January 1961, when his daughters were teenagers John separated from his wife, Marion, and she sued him for a divorce, which was finalised in July 1961.

Then, on the 10th May 1967, John married his 2nd wife Kate McNaught Murray (always called 'Kay'), John died on 3 January 1995 and Kay developed premature senility and she died a few years before him.

130. Ruth Frances Freemantle was the second child of Eric Freemantle and Phyllis Howard. She was born on 20 September 1928 in Jo-burg. She got married on 14 May 1949 at St Martins-in-the-Veld in Dunkeld, to Philip Alistair May. (*see extract later.*)

131. Lennox Roberts Freemantle was the third child, the elder of twins, born to Eric Freemantle and Phyllis Freemantle nee Howard. He was born in Johannesburg on 9 September 1934. At the time of his birth his parents were living in Orange Grove but they moved shortly to *'Graystones'*, 30, Eastwood Road, Dunkeld. The Rev. Pearson in the church of St Martins-in-the-Veld, Rosebank, christened the twins and they spent their childhood and youth at *'Graystones'*. Following on the twin's birth and a major operation, their mother's health deteriorated and a succession of European nursemaids were employed to assist during their early care.

On 10 May 1963 he married Joyce Roderick in Johannesburg. Their first home was in Edenvale and thereafter they moved to Bedfordview where they purchased a good-sized property. It was during the time he was with the firm that he bought a small game farm near Bandelier's Kop in the Northern Transvaal and spent all his spare time building this up and stocking it with animals.

They also own a holiday house in Oyster Bay, but Lennox's main interest in life, apart from his family, is in the small game farm, which after many years of hard work (and pleasure) finally began to make a profit. In 1988 Lennox left the firm of Pollak & Freemantle, Lennox then started his own stockbroking business in partnership with a Mr. Boner (a relation of Joyce's), calling it Boner & Freemantle.

Although they retained their home in Bedfordview, and he spent a good deal of his time at the farm, the family regularly enjoyed their holidays, especially over the Christmas period in Oyster Bay, in their holiday home, joining a number of other relatives of the Freemantle and Letty families, who also maintain holiday homes there.

132. Christopher Roberts Freemantle was the fourth child, the younger of twins, born to Eric Freemantle and Phyllis Freemantle nee Howard. He was born in Johannesburg on 9 September 1934.

At the time of his birth his parents were living in Orange Grove but they moved shortly to *'Graystones'*, 30, Eastwood Road, Dunkeld. The Rev. Pearson in the church of St Martins-in-the-Veld, Rosebank, christened the twins and they spent their childhood and youth at *'Graystones'*.

Following on the twin's birth and a major operation, their mother's health deteriorated and a succession of European nursemaids were employed to assist during their early care .

On 30 July 1960 in Johannesburg he married Beverley Coral Barnes; she was born on 2.10.1940. Christopher's career in the stock exchange started from being a messenger and clerk, through floor dealer and so on, culminating in his becoming Vice-President of the Johannesburg Stock Exchange in 1974-75 and President in 1976-77. He was elected a Life Member when he came to settle in the Cape in 1985.When he left Max Pollak & Freemantle he joined the Board of Executers in Cape Town living in the Constantia area while the children completed their education and then moved to Franschoek. It was some time after that, sadly, he cut off all ties with both his twin and the rest of the family.

133. Pamela Mary Freemantle was the eldest child of Ronald Roberts Freemantle and Constance Pauline Harrison. She was born on 16 December 1933 in Jo-burg, she married William Henry Morton Bradley on 23 April 1960 to William Henry Morton Bradley. She became a domestic Science teacher and he became an R.A.F. Electronics engineer.

i Mark Richard Bradley b. 10 February 1962, Aden.

ii Michael John Bradley b. 7 September 1963, Epping, Essex.

iii Martin David Bradley b. 8 January 1965, Cambridgeshire.

iv Karen Louise Bradley b. 5 December 1967, London.

v Anne Marie Bradley b. 10 November 1968, Saffron Weldon.

134. Paul Roberts Freemantle was the second child of Ronald Roberts Freemantle and Constance Pauline Harrison. He was born on 9 September 1935 and his parents were living in Mountain View at the time of his birth.

On leaving school he spent 10 years assisting his parents on their farm outside Lydenburg. Once it was decided to sell the farm, he went to Johannesburg.

On 26 February 1966 in Johannesburg he married Merle Williams, she was born in Johannesburg on 3 January 1935 Paul and Merle had two children, sadly, Merle died about three months after the birth of their daughter, Amanda, on 10 January 1969. Paul's parents accepted the responsibility of assisting him in the raising of these two babies during their infancy and moved into his home in order to do so. On 12 February 1972 in Jo-burg he married his 2nd wife, Magda Elizabeth Holm. Magda was born on 29 February 1944 and there were two children of this marriage, both daughters.

135. Owen George Freemantle was the third child Ronald Roberts Freemantle and Constance Pauline Freemantle nee Harrison. He was born on 11 July 1937 in Illovo, Johannesburg. On 11 December 1965 in Johannesburg he married Shonagh Mary Patricia MacRosty.

136. Ronald Joseph Freemantle was the fourth child of Ronald Roberts Freemantle and Constance Pauline Freemantle nee Harrison. Ronald was born on 17 May 1939 in Jo-burg and he married Margaretha Glen-Williams on 6 July 1963 in Jo-burg. She was born on 4 July 1942 in Lydenberg. He became a stockbroker.

137. Kenneth Freemantle was the only son of Charles Henry Freemantle and Nellie Florence Maud Rouse. Kenneth was born on 9 January 1920 in Bloemfontein. He worked for J.C.I.Co., [Johannesburg Consolidated Investment Company] for 41 years, being transferred many times during his career, and retired in 1978. On 14 July 1945 he married Barbara Trenbath, who was born on 16 February 1918 in Brakpan.

191 i   **Roger Freemantle**   b. 17 January 1951 in Johannesburg.
192 ii **Leanne Freemantle** b. 12 November 1958 in Johannesburg.

138. Thomas Jacobus Freemantle was the eldest child of George Richard Freemantle (2nd) and Emily Matilda Shaw. He was born 10 March 1933 in Uitenhage. He worked for the South African Railways and he married Sarah Gouws in Despatch on 14 December 1957. Sarah was born on 26 March 935).

139. George Richard Freemantle (VI) was the second child of George Richard Freemantle (2nd) and Emily Matilda Shaw. He was born on 19 October 1938 in Uitenhage. He worked for the South African Railways and he married Christina Wolfaard on 8 December 1962 in Port Elizabeth and they had four children.

140. Christina Maria Freemantle was the third child of George Richard Freemantle (2nd) and Emily Matilda Shaw. She was born 28 April 1932 in Uitenhage. When she was 20 years old she married Harry Thomas Jacobs on 14 April 1952. He was born on 19 January 1932 in Grahamstown and he was a Fitter and Turner.

141. Patricia Joan Freemantle was the fourth child of George Richard Freemantle (2nd) and Emily Matilda Shaw. She was b. 18 August 1935 in Uitenhage. She married on 12 December 1956 a Mr. van Loggerenberg. They had no children.

142. Jacobus Wilhelmus Freemantle (3rd), was the eldest son of Jacobus Wilhelmus Freemantle (2nd) and Sophia de Villiers. He was a warden.

143. Johannes Freemantle was the second son of Jacobus Wilhelmus Freemantle (2nd) and Sophia de Villiers. He was also a warden.
144. Sophia Freemantle was the third child of Jacobus Wilhelmus Freemantle (2nd) and Sophia de Villiers.
145. Andre Freemantle was the eldest child of Adriaan Frederick Freemantle and Wilhelmina Lodervika Coetzee. She was born 18 April 1947, in Johannesburg and he married Emmarentia Bosse; they had two children

146. Annet Freemantle was the second child of Adriaan Frederick Freemantle and Wilhelmina Lodervika Coetzee. She was born 1 January 1950 in Johannesburg, she married Winston Eva on 17 July 1981.

147. Riaan Freemantle was the third child of Adriaan Frederick Freemantle and Wilhelmina Lodervika Coetzee. He was born 17 July 1951 in Johannesburg. He married Ambelene Jenner and they had three children:

148. Deon Freemantle was the fourth child of Adriaan Frederick Freemantle and Wilhelmina Lodervika Coetzee. He was born on 17 July 1951 in Johannesburg.

149. Karen Freemantle was the fifth child of Adriaan Frederick Freemantle and Wilhelmina Lodervika Coetzee. b. 17 December 1960 and she married Jan Combrink.

150. Vivien May Freemantle was the eldest child of Johannes Jacobus (John) Freemantle and Dorothy May Kroezen. She was born on 26 June 1946 in Cape Town.
 She married on 10 August 1964 to William Anthony Douglas Adams. Douglas was born on 5 November 1943 in Durban. She worked as an accountant and he works for AGFA as a sales agent.

151. Charlotte Freemantle was the second child of Johannes Jacobus (John) Freemantle and Dorothy May Kroezen. She was born on 7 February 1948 in Cape Town and married there on 10 February 1973 to Anthony (Tony) Capp. He was born on 20 June 1947 in Essex, England. They emigrated to Australia shortly after their marriage.

152. John Freemantle was the third child of Johannes Jacobus (John) Freemantle and Dorothy May Kroezen. He was born on 6 March 1952 in Cape Town. He married Elizabeth Le Roux on 30 August 1978. Elizabeth was born on 12 June 1955. They have their own carpeting business in Fish Hoek.

153. Diane Freemantle was the fourth child of Johannes Jacobus (John) Freemantle and Dorothy May Kroezen. She was born on 18 October 1964 in Cape Town. She married Johan Janse van Rensburg. They later got divorced.

Children of Diane Freemantle and Johan Janse van Rensburg were:
  i Christopher Janse van Rensburg b. 18 September 1981
  ii James Janse van Rensburg b. 18 August 1985

154. Robert Daniele Freemantle was the eldest child of Robert Pienaar Freemantle and Johanna Maria (Joan) Kroezen. He was born 15 January 1950 in Cape Town, he married Marie Louise Hauker, who was born on 11 August 1955 in Cradock.

Children of Robert Daniele Freemantle and Marie Louise Hauker were:
  i**Robert John Freemantle** b. 21 September 1973

155. Michael Trevor Freemantle was the second child of Robert Pienaar Freemantle and Johanna Maria (Joan) Kroezen. He was born 20 August 1956 in Uitenhage.

156. Kathleen Joan Freemantle was the third child of Robert Pienaar Freemantle and Johanna Maria (Joan) Kroezen. She was born on 13 August 1956 in Uitenhage.

157. Julian Vernon Freemantle was the fourth child of Robert Pienaar Freemantle and Johanna Maria (Joan) Kroezen. He was born on 30 March 1962 in Vereeniging.

158. Susanna Elizabeth Susara Freemantle was the eldest child of Lynel Freemantle and Susanna Jakoba Petronella Koster. She was born on 6 February 1958 in Durban. She married Gilbert Jean-Jose D'oherty-Bigara, he was born on 19 February 1954.

159. Charmaine Amanda Maureen Freemantle was the second child of Lynel Freemantle and Susanna Jakoba Petronella Koster. She was born on 14 September 1959 in Durban. She married Louis Roets, he was born on 29 August 1957.

Children of Charmaine A. M. Freemantle and Louis Roets were:

    i   **Louis Roets** b. 2 December 1981 in Tzaneen
    ii   **Charmaine Eloise Roets** b. 12 March 1981 in Tzaneen.

160. Jacobus Johannes Freemantle was the third child of Lynel Freemantle and Susanna Jakoba Petronella Koster. He was born on 2 June 1961 in Durban and married Ingrid von Solms, she was born on 22 December 1962

161. Lionel Leslie Freemantle was the fourth child of Lynel Freemantle and Susanna Jakoba Petronella Koster. He was born on 18. April 1963 in Durban and married Rene Antoinette Wicks, she was born on 24 March 1966).

Children of Lionel Leslie Freemantle and Rene Antoinette Wicks were:

i   **Candice Rene Freemantle** b. 2 November 1984.
ii   **Lionel Vaughn Freemantle** b. 30 December 1985

162. Edmond Armand Freemantle was the fifth child of Lynel Freemantle and Susanna Jakoba Petronella Koster. He was born on 15 May 1968 in Durban.

163. Anthony Edwald Alain Freemantle was the sixth child of Lynel Freemantle and Susanna Jakoba Petronella Koster. He was born on 13 February 1972 in Durban.

164. Ronnie Winston Freemantle was the fourth child of Fred Wilfred Freemantle, and Emmerentia Bezuidenhout. He was born 15 August 1943. He married his 1st wife June Washer. Then, Ronnie Winston Freemantle married his 2nd wife Moyra Engelbrecht.

165. Victor Neville Freemantle was the eldest child of Clifford Walter Gordon Freemantle and Eileen Dorothy Cromhout. Victor was born 27 August 1939 in Kokstad and he became a Technical Fitter. On 18 April 1960 in Durban he married Phyllis Elizabeth Geithrie, who was born on 3 July 1937 in Durban.

166. Maureen Freemantle was the second child of Clifford Walter Gordon Freemantle and Eileen Dorothy Cromhout. She was born on 26 September 1941 at Flagstaff and died there on 2 January 1942 aged 3 months.

167. Lyle Myrtle Freemantle was the third child of Clifford Walter Gordon Freemantle and Eileen Dorothy Cromhout, She was born on 31 December 1943 in Port Shepstone and she married Colin Reginald Geithrie. He was born on 13 July 1942 in Durban and he was a locksmith.

168. David Llewellyn Freemantle was the fourth child of Clifford Walter Gordon Freemantle and Eileen Dorothy Cromhout, he was born on 5 September 1947 in Melmoth and he was also a locksmith. He married on 15 November 1968 Elizabeth Johanna Susanna Coetzee, who was born on 30 April 1952.

Children of David Llewellyn Freemantle and Elizabeth J. S. Coetzee were:

    i   **Steven Freemantle** b. 17 February 1969 in Durban.
    ii   **Gary Gordon Freemantle** b. 24 November 1970 Durban.

169. Michael Gordon Freemantle was the fifth child of Clifford Walter Gordon Freemantle and Eileen Dorothy Cromhout. Michael was born on 5 November 1948 at Eshowe and he became a technician. He married on 30 October 1968 in Durban Colleen Louise Fagan, who was born on 7 September 1951 in Durban.

170. George Arthur Freemantle was the sixth child of Clifford Walter Gordon Freemantle and Eileen Dorothy Cromhout. He was born on 29 April 1950 in Port Shepstone and died 2 days later on 1 May 1950, also in Port Shepstone.

171. Ivan Reginald Freemantle was the eldest son and the elder of twins born of Bertram Stanley Freemantle and Alicia P. Rosebrook. He was born on 29 December 1941 in Jo-burg. He was a Pharmacist and a Doctor (M.D.). He married Colleen Myfanwy Craig on 11 December 1965.

Children of Ivan Reginald Freemantle and Colleen Myfanwy Craig were:

    i   **Ian Duncan Freemantle** b. 10 May 1967 in Durban, Natal

    ii   **Lisa Colleen Freemantle** b. 29 July 1970 Durban, Natal

172. Aubrey Charles Freemantle was the second son and the younger of twins born of Bertram Stanley Freemantle and Alicia P. Rosebrook. He was born on 29 December 1941 in Jo-berg. He was a Doctor (M.D.) and a Pharmacist. He married Annie Steveart on 6 September 1968.

173. Stanley Walter Freemantle was the third son of Bertram Stanley Freemantle and Alicia P. Rosebrook. He was born on 10 September 1949 in Jo-burg. He was a Television Engineer. He married on 17 August 1975 in Durban, Beveley Barber.

174. Alfred Lionel Freemantle was the eldest child of Cecil Reginald Freemantle and Eva Duysel. He was born on 16 June 1948 Germiston, Tvl. He married on the 14 November 1974 Norma Avril McRobert

Children of Alfred Lionel Freemantle and Norma Avril McRobert were:

    i   **Clinton Lionel Freemantle** b. 26 October 1975 Germiston, Tvl
    ii **Andrew Murray Freemantle** b. 31 May 1974 Germiston, Tvl.

175. June Frances Freemantle was/is the eldest child **of John Mates Freemantle and Doris Rona Boshoff.**

She was born on 23 June 1949 in Cape Town. She married on the 6 of May her 1st husband Walter Duncanson Harper, but they eventually divorced.

She married her second husband Walter Henry Hugh Proctor on 26 June 1976.

Children of June Frances Freemantle and Walter Duncanson Harper were:

    i   Mark Steven Harper b. 31 October 1969
    ii Andrew Harper b. 12 December 1972

Children of June Frances Freemantle and Walter Henry Hugh Proctor were:

i   Mathew David Proctor b. 26 March 3.1978
ii Jared Daniel Proctor b. 26 June 1980
iii Jessica Louise Proctor b. 29 July 1983

176. John Christian Freemantle was/is the second child of **John Mates Freemantle and Doris Rona Boshoff.**

He was born on 20 August 1951 in Boksburg /Benoni. He married Susan Elizabeth Baker.

Children of John Christian Freemantle and Susan Elizabeth Baker were:
i   **Christian John Freemantle** b. 9 April 1978
ii **Daniel Peter Freemantle** b. 26 January 1980/1
iii **Michele Freemantle** b. 17 December 1983

177. Rosemary Dawn Freemantle is/was the third child of **John Mates Freemantle and Doris Rona Boshoff.**
She was born on 22 July 1953 in Boksburg/Benoni. She married on the 2nd of February Jacques Oliver.

Children of Rosemary Dawn Freemantle and Jacques Oliver were:
i   **Hayley Oliver** b. 22 June 1978
ii **Marc Oliver** b. January (?)
iii **Taryn Oliver**

178. David Michael Freemantle is/was the fourth child of **John Mates Freemantle and Doris Rona Boshoff.**
He was born on 14 November 1956 in Que Que, Rhodesia. He married on 31 March, to Karen Rene Casson.

Children of David Michael Freemantle and Karen Rene Casson were/are:

   i   **Nathan Alistair Freemantle** b. 19 June 1980
   ii **Angus Neville Freemantle** b. 31 December 1981
   iii **Alister Michael Freemantle** b. 19 January 1986
   iv **Kurt Freemantle** b. 16 January 1990

179. Robin Errol Freemantle was the fifth child of **John Mates Freemantle and Doris Rona Boshoff.**

He was born on 13 April 1958 in Que Que, Rhodesia, he married Ruelle ?.

Children of Robin Errol Freemantle and Ruelle Freemantle were:
   i   **Mathew Freemantle** b. 25 June 1986
   ii **Nicolas Freemantle** b. 14 February 1988

180. **Neil Paxton Freemantle** was the eldest son of Myles Paxton Freemantle and Gwenda Freemantle. He was born on 9 November 1957 in Cape Town. He married on 9 March 1988 at Kearsnay College Chapel, Botha's Hill, Durban, Natal Annamaria Di Paolo, she was born on 4 March 1956.

181. **James Paxton Freemantle** was the second son of Myles Paxton Freemantle and Gwenda Freemantle. He was born on 9 November 1959 in Jo-burg, he died on 6 October 1971 in Cape Town.

182. **Andrew Paxton Freemantle** was the third son of Myles Paxton Freemantle and Gwenda Freemantle. He was born on 12 June 1963 in Matatiele, East Griqualand.

Generation No. 7

183. Roderick John Freemantle; eldest son of Alric Joubert Freemantle and Patricia Bennett was born 12.10.1951 in Johannesburg. He married Elizabeth Goodwin.

Children of **Roderick John Freemantle and** Elizabeth Goodwin were:

    i   **Jonathan Paul Freemantle** born 16.6.1978.
    ii   **Matthew Alric Freemantle** born 7.3.1980.
    iii **Simon Arthur Christopher Freemantle** born 3 December 1982.

184. Richard Joubert Freemantle was the eldest child of Arthur Walter (Bob) Freemantle and Frances Josephine Letty. He was born on 19 August 1956, in Johannesburg. He married Sheila Guillard on 27 May 1979. She was born on 25 July 1952.

185. Diana Helen Freemantle was the second child of Arthur Walter (Bob) Freemantle and Frances Josephine Letty. She was born on 23 January 1959, in Johannesburg. She married Peter Weibel on 19 September 1981. He was born on 10 June 1956.

186. **Barbara Joan Freemantle** was the third child of Arthur Walter (Bob) Freemantle and Frances Josephine Letty. She was born on 7 February 1964, in Johannesburg.

Children of Paul Roberts Freemantle and Merle Williams were/are:

187. James (Jimmy) Roberts Freemantle was the eldest child of Paul Roberts Freemantle and Merle Williams. He was born on 23 April 1967 in Jo-burg. James completed his matric at Kloof High School and did his military training as soon as he left school. He studied engineering at Durban University after completion of his military training. He became a partner in a small electronics company. Jimmy married Dawn Grenfell, on 14.11.1992 in Kloof, Natal. Dawn was born on 13.12.1966.

188. Amanda Lee Freemantle was the second child of Paul Roberts Freemantle and Merle Williams. She was born on 26 October 1968 in Johannesburg. Mandy went into training for nursing as soon as she left school. She qualified as a staff nurse at the Entabeni Hospital in February 1989. Amanda married Charles Marshall, he was born on 5 April 1966 in Roodeport, Charles is an engineer and works for a very large company that makes tractors and earth moving equipment in Richards Bay.

Children of Paul Roberts Freemantle and Magda Elizabeth Holm were/are:

189. **Merle Louise Freemantle** was the third child of Paul Roberts Freemantle and the first of his 2nd marriage to Magda Elizabeth Holm. She was born on 4 January 1974 in Johannesburg. Merle qualified as a graphic designer and she married in Hillcrest, Natal on 26 March 2002 to Wayne Hodson.

190. Catherine Pauline Freemantle was the fourth child of Paul Roberts Freemantle and the second of his 2nd marriage to Magda Elizabeth Holm.

She was born on 31 December 1976. Catherine qualified in Marketing Management and she was married in Kloof, Natal on 21 August 2000 to Shaun Massey in 1999.

Shaun was born on 16 May 1973 in Durban, Natal. He and Catherine joined her parents in their business of 'Jumping Castles' and 'Highbury Function Hire' which hires out equipment required for functions of almost any kind.

They had a child born about March 2003.

191. Roger Freemantle, was the eldest child of Kenneth Freemantle and Barbara Freemantle nee Trenbath, he was born on 17 January 1951 in Johannesburg.

After school he completed his basic military training and worked, like his father, for J.C.I., where he became a Buyer.

However from there he moved on to S.A.B as a Computer User's Services manager.

On 12 April 1980 he was married to Marlene Gerna nee Otto in the Dutch Reformed Church, Halfway House, by ds. Van Staden.

Children of Roger Freemantle and Marlene Gerna nee Otto were/are:

    i   **Margeaux Freemantle** b. 14 May 1981, Sandton, Johannesburg

    ii **Carmen Freemantle** b. 28 August 1983, Sandton, Johannesburg.

192. Leanne Freemantle was the second child of Kenneth Freemantle and Barbara Freemantle nee Trenbath. She was born 0n 12 November 1958 in Johannesburg. She was baptised in the Anglican Church in Odendaalsrus, O.F.S.

On 14 July 1979, she married Anthony Santana, in Johannesburg, by the Rev. Richards. Leanne and Tony (as he is known) live in Halway House, where Leanne runs a successful Ladies Boutique. There are no children of this marriage.

Compiled by Serena de Jager. Any incorrections or additions please email sdj@itnet.co.za

Focusing on John Mates Freemantle and the connection to the City Of Fremantle, Western Australia.

(Extracts from Ruth Frances May (nee Freemantle) download)

It would seem that the connection between the family of Freemantle Settlers in 1820 and the Fremantle family of naval renown maybe somewhat closer than previously presumed, judging from the following extract taken from the 'Wynne Diaries', printed in 1937, and edited by Anne Fremantle.

These are the diaries of Elizabeth (Betsey) Wynne, [written from 1794 to 1798] who married Thomas Francis Fremantle (later Admiral Fremantle), father of the second Admiral Fremantle after whom the port in Western Australia is named, and her sister Eugenia Wynne.

Although nothing is confirmed and it is not known when the change of spelling might have taken place, she refers to Fremantle Park and Fremantle Farm, but the latter is spelt on the map as Freemantle and there is a Freemantle Park still in existence in Southampton.

When we visited Southampton in 1985 we were given to understand that there were in fact two parks there called Freemantle. However, we were only able to find one at that time during our rather hasty drive around the place.

CAPTAIN FREMANTLE'S FAMILY.

A synopsis (Appendix B) from the Wynne Diaries.
Volume II. 1794-1798.

The name Fremantle is found originally in Hampshire: Fremantle forest, North of Southampton, was a royal forest in Henry II's reign; at Fremantle Park, near Kingsclere (1) King John had a hunting box, where the Fremantle farm (2) still exists, supposedly on the ancient site. There is a present day suburb of Southampton named Fremantle as once there was also of Bournemouth (now swallowed up by the encroaching city).

The earliest direct ancestor of Betsy's husband of whom there is any authentic record, left his native county to become agent to Lord Crewe, the then prime bishop of Durham, in 1660. Lord Crewe had an estate near Stean, (3) in the neighbourhood of Brackley, (4) and John Fremantle (who in the grant of arms to his grandson is described as 'of the county of Hants') lived at Morton Pinkney, (5) and is buried there. He is mentioned in one volume of Evleyn's diary, in connection with the Northamptonshire floods, and it is permissible to suppose it was his father whom Scott describes in the preface to 'Woodstock', as being at Leckhampstead, (6) near Buckingham.

John Fremantle had three sons and one daughter. The latter married one Cunningham, and is buried at Brackley. (7) Of the boys, the eldest Thomas, was a graduate of Lincoln College, Oxford, and later became rector of Hinton in the Hedges, (8) near Aynhoe. (9) He died childless.

The second, John, went merchanting abroad, and was living in Lisbon in 1703. The third, Walgrave (a Crewe name - no doubt bestowed by a beneficent godfather), married and lived and died in Morton Pinkney, (10) and his descendants after him remained there until the nineteenth century, undistinguished and undisturbed.
John, who went to Lisbon, married there Catherine Carter. Family tradition has it that the great earthquake, which destroyed Francois-Marie Arout's faith in the benevolence of his creator, destroyed also the record of John Fremantle's marriage. At all events, the family Bible still in the possession of his descendants gives the date of his first child, Maria, as 1703; John followed in 1705.
This John (the second) grew up in Portugal, then crossed over into Spain and became secretary of legation at Madrid, and married a Spanish lady, remarkable for her extreme youth and even more extreme ugliness, one Maria Teresa de Castro.
They were married in her parent's house, but not in their presence, which gave rise to the legend that John had eloped with her from a convent. Certainly she had taken neither vows nor veil, but she may still have been at school.
John and Maria had first a daughter, Frances, and then, on June 21, 1737, John (the third), who bought an estate at Aston Abbotts, (11) near Aylesbury, (12) and married an heiress, Frances Edwards. She brought other gifts, too, than money: long black lashes all her descendants inherit, and dark hazel - almost green - eyes, and, alas, pigstraight dark hair.
Frances' and John's eldest son John, born 1761, went

into the Guards and died in 1805 at Bath, childless. He was buried at Melksham, (13) but there is a tablet to his memory in Bath Abbey. Sara, the next child, born in 1762, married Lord Cathcart's son, Archibald.

Then came Stephen, born in 1764. He became lieutenant-colonel of the 39th. Infantry in 1786, and in 1794 married Albinia Jeffreys. Their son, John, was in 1818 aide-de-camp to the Duke of Wellington, and his descendant, Guy Fremantle, the last representative of this branch of the family, now lives at Alassio (14).

Thomas Francis, the hero of this volume, was born at 9 a.m. one morning in 1765. After him came his younger brother, William Henry, in 1766. These two brothers were always very intimate, and when Thomas Francis died in 1819 William took care of young Tom, his nephew, who, as he was already of age, needed no legal guardian.

When he died he left Tom all his money, and some Edwards property, too, near Bristol. William was for eleven years permanent secretary for Ireland, and member for Bucks.

He married (as Betsy so graphically describes) Selina, relict of Felton Hervey. Later he became deputy ranger of Windsor Great Park, and her father-in-law could remember his grandfather telling him how he used, as a boy, to go over from Eton to Holly Grove (15) in '42 and visit his uncle, and how the old servant used to brush his uncle's wig on a stand.

More info:

FF 6d *SAMUEL FREEMANTLE'S FAMILY (continued)

F6/4.9Fa Oliver Woodland Freemantle   = (1st) Muriel Selina Goldsmith
             (1879 - 1949)   [m. 1907]   (1882
-    )
                                         = (2nd) Dorothy Frances Mates
                              [m. 1920]   (1893 -
1959)

Oliver Woodland Freemantle was the sixth child of **Jesse William Freemantle** and **Fanny Elizabeth Freemantle nee Paxton** and the grandchild of

* Samuel Freemantle and ***Sarah Freemantle nee Paxton.**

 He was born in the Transkei, possibly in Umtata, on 18.2.1879 and grew up in that town. [IGI has his birthplace as Elliot, Cape and this may well be correct]

He was on the Post Office staff in Fort Beaufort, Cape, at the time of his first marriage on 25.9.1907, when he married **Muriel Selina Goldsmith.** She was born in 1882 and they were divorce in 1920 after 13 years of marriage. There was one child of this union:

F6/5.F[A]Theodore Eileen Muriel Freemantle   - unfortunately, no details of her life have been traced.

On 9.12.1920 in Wynberg, Cape, **Oliver Woodland Freemantle** married **(2ⁿᵈ) Dorothy Frances Mates.**

She was born on 26.8.1893 in Arendal, Sussex, England and died on 16.8.1959, at the time of this marriage he was working in the Public Roads Department in Cape Town. Later, he also became a Divisional Council Engineer.

There were five children of this second marriage. He died on 18.1.1949 and his widow survived him by ten years, dying on 16.8.1959 in Cape Town.

Oliver Woodland Freemantle and **Dorothy Frances Mates also had a son:**

F6/5.F.[B] John Mates Freemantle
　　　　　　b. 12. 3.1922 Cape Town
　　　　　m. 29.11.1947 Pinelands, Cape

　　　　　　Doris Rona Boshoff, daughter of the Assistant Manager of Railways. Hendrick Christiaan Boshoff
　　　　　　b. 5. 3. 1927 Pretoria, Transvaal

5 children - see separate section **F6/5.F.[B] John Mates = D.R Boshoff.**

See previous material re children.

F6/5.F.[B] John Mates Freemantle = Doris Rona Boshoff
(1922 -   )   [m. 1947]   (1927 -   )

John Mates Freemantle was the eldest son and the first born child of Oliver Woodland Freemantle's second marriage. His mother was Dorothy Frances Freemantle nee Mates. He was born on 12.3.1922 in Cape Town.

On 29.11.1947 he married **Doris Rona Boshoff**, daughter of **Hendrik Christian Boshoff and Eva Cecily Boshoff nee Gibson,** who was born in Albany, Western Australia. Her father was John Gibson, a Scot. The Gibson family went to South Africa when Eva was about 10 years old. She died in 1974, in East London, Cape Province, South Africa.

Her father was the Assistant Manager of Railways. They were married in Pinelands, Cape, and **John Mates Freemantle** became a stationmaster. Eventually **John and Doris Freemantle** emigrated from South Africa and went to live in Perth, Australia, after many years in Northern Rhodesia.

They now live in a retirement village in Mandurah, Western Australia.

Doris was one of 11 children, and sister to my father, **Louis Edwin Boshoff.**

Lesley Moseley

www.ingramcontent.com/pod-product-compliance
Lightning Source LLC
Chambersburg PA
CBHW072209280526
45788CB00002B/942